God's Great & Precious Promises

Connie Witter

HENSLEY
PUBLISHING

About Photocopying This Book

I Timothy 5:17-18 instructs us to give the laborer his wages, specifically those who labor in the Word and doctrine. Hensley Publishing has a moral, as well as legal, responsibility to see that our authors receive fair compensation for their efforts. Many of them depend upon the income from the sale of their books as their sole livelihood. So for that matter, do the artists, printers, and numerous others people who work to make these books available to you. Please help us by discouraging those who would copy this material in lieu of purchase.

God's Great and Precious Promises

ISBN 1-56322-063-6

Dedication

I dedicate this Bible study to my Lord and Savior Jesus Christ. I'm so thankful for all He has done for me.

I'm also grateful for the commission He has given me, my husband Tony, and Neal and Sherry Hensley to publish this good news of the gospel all over the world.

The Lord gave the word: great was the company of those that published it.
Psalm 68:11 KJV

Acknowledgments

If it weren't for the grace of God, I would never have been able to write this Bible study. The Holy Spirit has guided me to the truth I'm sharing with you, and that has changed my life and set me free. The truth found in this Bible study has brought increased measures of faith, joy, and peace in my life. I'm so thankful to God for using me to share with others how they, too, can live the victorious Christian life.

I'm blessed to have a husband who prays for me and encourages me to fulfill God's plan for my life. I couldn't fulfill the call of God on my life without his love and support.

I want to thank my first Bible study group, Sherry Hensley, Nancy Fite, and Kelly Reed. They were faithful to sit through this teaching many times as the Holy Spirit continued to help me organize it into manuscript form. God has blessed my life with their friendships. They're all living testimonies of how God's promises can change your life when you put your absolute trust in them.

I especially want to thank my wonderful friend Sherry Hensley for encouraging me to publish this study. She has spent many hours reading and typing each lesson, and has also given me much help in writing them. Without her vision and encouragement, this book would never have been completed. She's one of God's greatest blessings in my life.

Finally, I want to thank my mother-in-law, Barb Witter, for editing the manuscript. I'm very grateful to her for the time she spent going over each lesson to make sure it was ready for publication.

Table of Contents

Introduction

As Christians, when we find ourselves facing a problem, we often hear people encouraging us to "put your trust in God." Do, you ever wonder:

- How do I trust God?
- Is He trustworthy? (Can I *really* trust Him?)
- How can I learn to trust Him more?
- What has He promised concerning my situation?
- How can I receive all that He has promised me?

In this Bible study, you'll discover the answer to all of these questions. You'll learn about the wonderful plan God has for your life. You'll study the great and precious promises He has given you through Jesus Christ. And you'll learn how to trust Him to bring them to pass in your life.

When we face a problem in life, God always responds with a promise. As you read God's Word you'll discover that the Bible is full of people, just like you, who faced trials. Men and women of the Bible such as Abraham, Sarah, Joseph, David, Caleb, Joshua, King Jehoshaphat, Paul, the lady with the issue of blood (Matthew 9:18-26), a blind man (Mark 8:22-26), a crippled woman (Luke 13:10-17), and many others faced difficult circumstances, and many times impossible situations. But, they each put their trust in a promise of God and every one of them came through their trial victoriously. In this Bible study, you'll learn how you can follow their examples and live a life of victory by trusting in the promises of God.

Many people have taught, and many people have believed, that God doesn't always deliver us out of our problem when we put our trust in Him. But that's not what the Bible tells us. The apostle Paul, who faced many trials, had this to say: *Persecutions, sufferings — what kinds of things happened to me in Antioch, Iconium and Lystra, the persecutions I endured. Yet the Lord rescued me **from all of them*** (II Timothy 3:11 — NIV). In II Peter 2:9 (NIV), Peter said *the Lord knows how to rescue godly men from trials.* And in Psalm 34:19, David said *a righteous man may have many troubles, but the Lord delivers him **from them all.*** (NIV)

At one time or another you'll face problems in your life. But no matter what problem you face (marital, financial, health, persecution, temptation, difficult relationships, problems with your children, etc.), you'll find God's answer for you in His Word. As you learn about the promises God has given you, and as you begin to put your trust in them, He will bring you victoriously through every challenging situation. The key is to realize that God's Word is your source of strength and to hold on to His promises in every trying circumstance — no matter how impossible it may seem. It's the only way to truly be successful and live a victorious Christian life.

Don't allow the teachings of men, the experiences of others, your own impossible situation, or your own reasoning to cause you to doubt God's promises. Many of His people will never experience His perfect will for their life because they believe the word of man more than the Word of God.

I encourage you to become like God's people in Acts 17:11. They searched the Scriptures daily to make sure that what they were being taught was true. Allow the Holy Spirit to be your teacher and He will guide you to the truth that will set you free. You'll experience God's supernatural ability in your life when you put your absolute trust in His Word.

It's my prayer that, as you study God's Word, the eyes of your understanding will be opened to all that belongs to you through Christ Jesus. I pray that you'll come to know and understand the immeasurable, unlimited and surpassing greatness of God's power — power which works in your life when you choose to believe His Word. I also pray that your faith won't rest in the wisdom of man, but rather, in the power of God! (Ephesians 1:17-19 and I Corinthians 2:4-5)

All things are possible to him that believeth. Mark 9:23 (KJV)

Connie Witter

Guidelines for Study

A. Guidelines for Individual Study

1. Make a commitment to finish the whole Bible study. It's very easy to become side-tracked, so set aside a quiet time every day to be alone with God and study His Word.

2. Each day before you begin to study, pray and ask God to give you a clear understanding of the Scriptures. As you do this, the Holy Spirit will be your teacher. He will guide you into all truth (John 16:13) and, through God's Word, He will reveal God's perfect will for your life.

3. Each lesson will take approximately one hour to complete unless you decide to read every scripture reference. Looking up each verse is optional, but very beneficial.

4. From the following plans, choose the one that best fits your schedule:

   a. Option 1. Do one lesson each week. Set aside one hour to complete the lesson. Then, throughout the week, continue to read over the same lesson several times. By doing this, you'll get the most from God's Word.

      • Divide lessons 4-7 into two lessons each. Complete Roman Numeral I the first week, and Roman Numeral II the following week.

      • If you choose this plan, it's important that you dedicate an entire week to each lesson so you can memorize and meditate on the Scriptures in the Personal Application. According to the *Amplified Bible*, Mark 4:24 says that the amount of thought and study you give to the truth you hear will determine the amount of revelation knowledge and spiritual strength that you'll receive from God's Word.

   b. Option 2. Divide each lesson into two 30-minute sessions by doing Roman Numeral I in the first session, and Roman Numerals II & III in a separate session. Lessons 8, 13, & 14 don't have sections, so divide these lessons in half according to the number of pages. For example, if a lesson has 10 pages, complete five pages in the first session and the remaining five the in the next session. After completing each part, reread the whole lesson.

      • If you choose this option, it's still important to complete one entire lesson before proceeding to the next lesson. Studying God's Word is more than just reading. It's taking time to think about the Scriptures, and allowing them to enter into your heart. When God's Word enters your heart, it will change your life.

   c. Option 3. Use this Bible study as a 15 minute devotional by completing two pages a day. Each lesson is 9-13 pages long, so by doing this, you'll complete one lesson each week.

5. Do the Personal Application. It's very important. The Bible instructs us to be doers of the Word and not hearers only (James 1:22-25). The Personal Application is designed to help you apply the truths from each lesson to your own life. Memorize the Scriptures in this section before proceeding to the next lesson. If you want God's Word to enter your heart, you must take the time to memorize and meditate on the Scriptures.

B. Guidelines for Group Study.

1. Set a specific time each week to get together and study God's Word. Have one person lead the group.

2. Begin each study with prayer. Ask God for a clear understanding of His Word. Ephesians 1:17-19 would be a good prayer for your group.

3. From the following plans choose the one that best fits your group's schedule. It will take approximately 90 minutes to go through one whole lesson in a group study.

   a. Divide lessons 4-7 into two lessons each. Complete Roman Numeral I the first week, and Roman Numeral II the following week. If you choose this plan, it will take your group 18 weeks to complete this study.

   b. If you don't have 90 minutes, divide each lesson into two 45-minute sessions by doing Roman Numeral I one week and Roman Numerals II & III the following week. Lessons 8, 13, & 14 don't have Roman Numerals, so if you can't complete them in 45 minutes, divide these lessons in half according to the number of pages. For example, if a lesson has 10 pages, complete five pages one week and the remaining five the following week. Following this example, your group will complete this study in 28 weeks.

4. Take turns reading the scriptures and answering the questions. Take time to discuss each question as a group, but avoid getting off track with side issues.

5. Assign the next week's lesson as homework. Encourage everyone to study it throughout the week. If students wait until the last minute to review the lesson, they won't get the most from God's Word. Acts 17:11 says that the wisest of God's people will study His Word daily.

6. Encourage all students to complete the Personal Application section of each lesson. Discuss the answers to the review questions. If your study group is small, have the students quote the scriptures they memorized. If your group is larger, select 2-3 volunteers to quote the scriptures. Take time to discuss the situations in the Personal Application section of each lesson. Select 2-3 volunteers from your group to share their situations and the promises they have found in God's Word that give them hope. It's important to encourage one another with God's Word.

Lesson 1
God's Plan for You Is Abundant Life

PURPOSE

To learn about God's plan for you and to realize He has given you great and precious promises so you can live a victorious Christian life.

OVERVIEW

God wants you to live a life of victory. He has proven this by what He has promised in His Word. It has a promise for every problem. When you experience trials and troubles in your life, you can have joy and peace that passes all understanding — if you'll learn to focus your heart and mind on God's Word and what He has promised there. When you put your absolute trust in a promise from God, you'll come through every trial victoriously and you'll walk in abundant life.

DISCUSSION

I. God's plan for you is revealed in His Word.

John 10:10 says: *The thief comes only in order that he may steal and may kill and may destroy. I came that they may have and enjoy life, and have it in abundance — to the full, till it overflows.* (AMP)

Write exactly what Jesus says He came to give you:_____

_____

_____

What does it mean to have life "in abundance"? By studying the meaning of original Greek words used in Scripture, we can gain a greater understanding of the life that Jesus came to give us. The original Greek word translated "abundance" in this scripture is *perissos*.

Perissos means:

- superabundant (in quantity)
- exceeding abundantly above
- superior (in quality)
- beyond measure

According to the Greek, then, how would you describe the following aspects of the life of a person who's experiencing life "in abundance"?

Their spiritual life:_____

_____

_____

5

Their emotional life:_____
_____
_____

Their marriage:_____
_____
_____

Their health:_____
_____
_____

Their finances:_____
_____
_____

Ephesians 3:20 is the only other verse of scripture in which the Greek word *perissos* is used. Here it again describes the abundant life that Jesus came to give you. *Now to Him Who, by (in consequence of) the [action of His] power that is at work within us, is able to [carry out His purpose and] do superabundantly, far over and above all that we [dare] ask or think — infinitely beyond our highest prayers, desires, thoughts, hopes or dreams.* (AMP)

What are your highest prayers, hopes and dreams? Take a moment to write down the desires of your heart._____
_____
_____
_____
_____

Personalize Ephesians 3:20 so you can better understand what God wants you to experience in your life. How much more does God want for you compared to what you want for yourself?_____
_____
_____
_____
_____

Does this scripture give you a better understanding of the life Jesus came to give you? Explain. _____
_____

Jesus came so that you can have a life that's superabundant in quantity, superior in quality and exceeding abundantly above and beyond measure. Deuteronomy 28:1-13 clearly reveals that God wants you to be blessed in every area of your life. Ephesians 3:20 tells us that

God is able to carry out His purpose for you — superabundantly, far over and above your highest prayers, desires, thoughts, hopes or dreams. He wants you to live a victorious Christian life by experiencing victory in every situation. Had you realized your Heavenly Father has such a wonderful plan for you?

John 10:10 contrasts the difference between the devil's desire for you (to steal, to kill, and to destroy) and God's will for you (to have abundant life). Numerous scriptures in the Bible describe God's will for His people. It's always the exact opposite of what the devil wants.

God's will for you includes:

- victory (I Corinthians 15:57)
- peace (John 14:27)
- health (Proverbs 4:20-22)
- love (II Timothy 1:7)
- protection (Psalm 91)
- joy (John 17:13)
- abundance (II Corinthians 9:6-11)
- success (Joshua 1:8)
- spiritual growth (Colossians 1:9-12)

These qualities will be evident in the life of the believer who's living the abundant life Jesus came to give. God wants these qualities to be evident in your life!

The devil's desires for you include:

- defeat (I Peter 5:8)
- worry and fear (II Timothy 1:7)
- jealousy and selfishness (James 3:14-15)
- sickness (Luke 13:10-16; Acts 10:38)
- poverty (Proverbs 10:15; I Peter 5:8)
- discouragement (Psalm 42:9-11)
- failure (John 10:10)
- bondage to sin (Ephesians 2:1-2)
- harm (Ephesians 6:11-18)

I John 3:8 teaches us that Jesus destroyed all the works of the devil. Jesus has redeemed us from each one of these characteristics. He did this so we can experience the blessings of Abraham in every area of our life (Galatians 3:13-14).

Jeremiah 29:11 describes the plan God has for His people: *"For I know the plans I have for you," declares the Lord, "plans to prosper you and not to harm you, plans to give you hope and a future."* (NIV)

Explain God's plan for you according to this scripture. _____
_____
_____

This scripture clearly states that it's **never** God's plan to bring harm into your life.

Exactly what does *harm* mean? The original Hebrew word found in Jeremiah 29:11 is *ra* which means:

- bad
- calamity
- evil
- grief
- adversity
- harm
- affliction
- trouble

So, Jeremiah 29:11 clearly tells us that it's never God's plan for us to experience evil, adversity, calamity or harm. Although God's people have experienced these things, according to this verse, it's not His will for them. James 1:12-13, 16-17 state: *12Blessed is the man who perseveres under trial.... 13When tempted, no one should say, "God is tempting me." For God cannot be tempted by evil, nor does he tempt anyone. 16Don't be deceived, my dear brothers. 17Every good and perfect gift is from above, coming down from the Father of the heavenly lights, who does not change like shifting shadows.* (NIV)

What does verse 13 tell you that you should never say when you're experiencing trials? Why?_____

_____

_____

What warning does God's Word give you in verse 16? According to verse 17, what truth should you believe about your Heavenly Father?_____

_____

_____

According to this passage of scripture, does harm, sickness, tragedy or adversity come from God?_____What does come from God?_____

_____

It's very easy to distinguish the sources of good and evil. Every good and perfect gift you ever receive comes from your Heavenly Father. He doesn't change the way shadows do as the sun moves across the sky, nor does His will change. He's the author of life, peace, joy, love, health, prosperity and victory. He's never the author of evil. Never make the mistake of blaming God for the work that the devil does. (John 10:10)

Some Christians teach that God brings trials into people's lives — trials such as illness, temptation, harm, etc. Indeed, there are many references to the fact that, under the old covenant, God poured His wrath and anger upon His people because of their sins. However, God sent His Son Jesus to take the sins of the whole world, and the consequences of sin, upon Himself (Isaiah 53:5-12). Because of this, we who accept Jesus as our Lord and Savior are no longer bound under God's wrath and anger. In Isaiah 54:9-10 God says: *"So now I have sworn not to be angry with you, never to rebuke you again. Though the mountains be shaken and the hills be removed, yet my unfailing love for you will not be shaken nor my covenant of peace be removed," says the Lord, who has compassion on you.* (NIV) Romans 5:8-9 says that we've been saved from God's wrath through Jesus Christ. And Galatians 3:13-14 clearly tells us that Jesus redeemed us from the curses of the law — sickness, harm, lack, depression, defeat (Deuteronomy 28:15-67) — so that the blessings promised to Abraham — health, protection, abundance, joy, victory — can be ours (Deuteronomy 28:1-13). We have entered into a new and better covenant — a covenant in which only that which is good comes from God's hand.

James 1:16-17 warns us not to be deceived into believing anything contrary to this truth from God's Word.

Psalm 35:27 tells us what God desires for His people: *Let those who favor my righteous cause and have pleasure in my uprightness shout for joy and be glad, and say continually, Let the Lord be magnified, Who takes pleasure in the prosperity of His servant.* (AMP)

What gives God pleasure? What does God want for you?_____

_____

_____

The word *prosper* in Jeremiah 29:11, and the word *prosperity* in Psalm 35:27 are derivatives of the Hebrew word *shalom*. Learning the meaning of this word will help you better understand God's will for your life.

Shalom means:

- safe
- happy
- welfare
- prosperity

- well
- friendly
- health
- peace

According to this definition then, what does God mean when He says in Jeremiah 29:11 that His plan is to prosper you?_____

_____

_____

God delights in your safety, happiness, welfare and good health. It gives Him pleasure when you experience peace and prosperity — spiritually, mentally, emotionally, physically and financially. You're His child and He's your Father (Romans 8:14-16). He wants the best for you. Matthew 7:11 states: *If you then, evil as you are, know how to give good and advantageous gifts to your children,* **how much more** *will your Father Who is in heaven [perfect as He is] give good and advantageous things to those who keep on asking Him!* (AMP)

Think about all that you want for your own children. If you could provide them, what characteristics would be evident in their lives?_____

_____

_____

_____

Matthew 7:11 clearly reveals that God wants all this, and more, for you!

In III John 2 we can again see what God wants for His people: *Beloved, I wish above all things that thou mayest prosper and be in health, even as thy soul prospers* (KJV).

Personalize this verse. What does God want for you above all things?_____

_____

_____

II. God has given you great and precious promises so you can walk in the abundant life He has planned.

Read II Peter 1:3-4: *3His divine power has given us everything we need for life and godliness through our knowledge of him who called us by his own glory and goodness. 4Through these he has given us his very great and precious promises, so that through them you may participate in the divine nature and escape the corruption in the world caused by evil desires.* (NIV)

What has God's divine power given you?

verse 3:_____

verse 4:_____

God has given you everything you need to live a victorious Christian life through your knowledge of Jesus, who is the Word of God (John 1:1, 14). The Bible contains promises that will bring you victory in every area of your life. As you grow in the knowledge of Jesus and His Word, you'll begin to understand the great and precious promises that are yours because of Him. God has given you promises for eternal life, forgiveness of sin, healing, answered prayer and deliverance. Through your faith in Jesus Christ, you've inherited promises of life, peace, joy, restoration, prosperity, victory and protection, because you are a child of God (II Corinthians 1:20).

According to II Peter 1:4, why did God give you such great and precious promises?

_____

_____

God wants you to participate in His nature. He wants you to have His peace, His joy, His righteousness and His love operating in your life. He gave you His promises so you can escape the consequences of sin. He wants you to live a life of victory by receiving all that He has promised.

Read I Timothy 4:8: *For bodily exercise profiteth little: but godliness is profitable unto all things, having promise of the life that now is, and of that which is to come.* (KJV)

Why is godliness profitable?_____

_____

Godliness is profitable because you inherit not only the promise of spending eternity in heaven with Jesus, but also all of His blessings and promises for your life on earth. God's Word contains thousands of promises. If you want to receive all He has planned for you, don't neglect or reject any of them. When you begin to put your complete trust in God's every promise, you'll live a life of victory.

III. When you experience trials and troubles, you can find the answers you need in God's Word.

God has given you many promises that offer hope in every situation. Although His will for you is abundant life, and His plan is to prosper you, there will still be times when you'll go through trials or experience trying circumstances. When you face difficult situations, look to God's Word for the answers to your problems. His promises cover every need you'll ever have. If you're willing to search His Word, He'll direct you to the answers and you'll walk in abundance. When you focus your heart and mind on what He has promised, you'll experience victory in every situation.

Learn how to live a life of victory by examining the lives of men who looked to God's promises when they encountered problems. You can find examples of victorious living throughout the Bible.

From I Samuel 30:1-26, we learn that an army had burned King David's city and stolen his wife, children, and all of his possessions. Problems surrounded him, and David was greatly distressed. Still, in the midst of his trial, he looked to God for his answer.

I Samuel 30:8 says God promised David: *Pursue; for you shall surely overtake them, and without fail recover all.* (AMP)

Immediately, David found hope in God's promise. He trusted in the Word God had spoken and, just as God had promised, he recovered all. He came through his trial victoriously because he chose to put his trust in God.

We see another example in John 4:46-53. A nobleman, or royal official, had a son who was very sick. This father had heard of the miracles of Jesus, and he knew that Jesus was the answer. He went to Jesus for the solution to his problem.

John 4:50 tells us Jesus gave the man a promise: *Go in peace; your son will live! And the man put his trust in what Jesus said and started home.* (AMP)

When Jesus gave the royal official a promise, the official immediately trusted in the word that Jesus had spoken. He was confident that his son would live because of what Jesus had promised him. His son was healed, and he received victory in his situation because he focused his heart and mind on the promise that God had given him.

If David and the royal official hadn't looked to God's promise in the midst of their trials, how would their stories be different? Would they have received God's plan for their lives?

_____

_____

You can see another example of a person looking to God's promise in the midst of trouble in Psalm 119:81-82: 81*I faint for your salvation; but I expect your help, for you have promised it.* 82 *My eyes are straining to see your promises come true.* (TLB)

What did the Psalmist expect? Why? What was he waiting for?_____

_____

_____

Look at Psalm 119:49-50: 49*Never forget your promises to me your servant, for they are my only hope.* 50 *They give me strength in all my troubles; how they refresh and revive me!* (TLB)

What was the Psalmist's only hope in the midst of his troubles?_____
_____

What did God's promises give him?_____
_____

Do you draw your strength from God's promises when you face difficult situations? Are God's promises your only source of hope?

You may face many problems in life:

- problems in your marriage
- strife
- temptations
- difficult situations with your children
- unsaved family and friends
- fear

- sickness in your home
- difficult relationships
- financial problems
- problems on your job
- discouragement

What problem have you been facing in your life? Write down an area of your life in which you've been facing difficult circumstances._____
_____
_____
_____

Just as David and the royal official put their trust in a promise that God had given them, you, too, must look to God's Word for a promise in which you can put your trust. God has promised He will deliver you out of every problem you face.

Psalm 34:17-19 says: 17*The righteous cry out, and the Lord hears them; he delivers them from all their troubles.* 18*The Lord is close to the brokenhearted and saves those who are crushed in spirit.* 19*A righteous man may have many troubles, but the Lord delivers him from them all.* (NIV)

From which troubles does God say He will deliver you? What promise has He given you in these verses, concerning the problem you are facing?_____
_____
_____
_____

Although God doesn't promise that you'll never face trials and troubles, *He does promise to deliver you out of them all!* He has promised victory in every situation to those who choose to put their absolute trust in His power, wisdom and goodness (Psalm 37:39-40).

Read Psalm 9:9-10: 9 *The Lord also will be a refuge and a high tower for the oppressed, a refuge and a stronghold in times of trouble....* 10*And they who know Your name...will lean on and confidently put their trust in you; for you, Lord, have not forsaken those who seek (inquire of and for You) [on the authority of God's Word and the right of their necessity].* (AMP)

What hope can you find in these verses when you face problems in your own life? Why can you draw your strength from the promise found in verse 10?_____

_____

_____

_____

Psalm 9:9-10 reveals how you can receive victory in every area of your life. Take a closer look at the truths found in these verses.

- God is your Refuge. He'll be your Stronghold in times of trouble.
- When you know your Heavenly Father, you'll lean on Him, and confidently put your trust in Him.
- He'll never fail to help you when you seek Him on the authority of His Word.

What does it mean to seek God on the authority of His Word? Simply put, it means to search God's Word for the answers you need to the problems and situations in your life. God's Word contains all the promises, counsels and commands you'll ever need to bring victory over temptations, tests and trials.

I Thessalonians 2:13 says God's Word is able to exercise its supernatural power in your life if you'll choose to trust in it: *And we also [especially] thank God continually for this, that when you received the message of God [which you heard] from us, you welcomed it not as the word of [mere] men but as what it truly is, the Word of God, which is effectually at work in you who believe — exercising its [superhuman] power in those who adhere to and trust in and rely on it.* (AMP)

According to this scripture, what must you do in order for God's Word to do a powerful work in your life?_____

_____

If you want to receive the wonderful plans God has for you, you must be willing to seek Him on the authority of His Word. When you adhere to, trust in and rely upon God's Word and the promises He has given you, you'll experience victory in every area of your life.

SUMMARY

God's Word reveals that His plan for you includes life, peace, joy, love, prosperity, success, health and victory. He sent His Son Jesus so that you could have a life of superior quality. Sickness, depression, lack, failure and defeat are never God's will for your life; the Bible makes it very clear that these come from the devil. When you experience circumstances that are contrary to God's will, you can receive victory by putting your trust in the promises of His Word. His Word contains everything you need to live a victorious Christian life. If you're willing to seek God on the authority of His Word, then you'll receive the wonderful plan He has for you.

PERSONAL APPLICATION

Mark 4:24 says: *the measure [of thought and study] you give [to the truth you hear] will be the measure [of virtue and knowledge] that comes back to you, and more [besides] will be given to you who hear.* (AMP)

This scripture says that the amount of thought and study you give to the truth you hear will determine the amount of knowledge and spiritual strength you receive from God's Word. If you want to live a victorious Christian life, you must take time every day to meditate on God's Word and memorize scriptures.

Romans 12:2 says: *Be ye transformed by the renewing of your mind, that ye may prove what is that good, and acceptable, and perfect, will of God.* (KJV)

When you renew your mind to the truth of God's Word, you prove to yourself what God's will is for you.

Begin to renew your mind with the scriptures you've learned in this lesson. The following scriptures are paraphrased and personalized so you can better apply them to your life.

1. John 10:10: The thief came to steal, kill, and to destroy, but Jesus came so I can have and enjoy life, and have it in abundance.

2. Ephesians 3:20: According to the power of God that is at work in my life, He is able to do superabundantly far over and above all that I ask or think — infinitely beyond my highest prayers, desires, thoughts, hopes and dreams.

3. Jeremiah 29:11: I know the plans God has for me. He has plans to prosper me and not to harm me — plans to give me hope and a future.

4. II Peter 1:4: God has given me great and precious promises so I can live a victorious Christian life.

5. Psalms 119:49-50: God's promises give me strength in all my troubles. They are my only source of hope.

REVIEW QUESTIONS

1. According to definition of the original Greek word translated "abundance," describe the life Jesus came to give you._____

   _____

2. Recall the meaning of the original Greek word translated "prosper," and describe the plan God has for your life. _____

   _____

3. What did God give you so you can live a life of victory? (II Peter 1:4)

   _____

   _____

4. What did David and the royal official do that brought them victory in their situations?

   _____

   _____

5. When you experience difficult situations, from where should you draw your strength? What should be your source of hope?_____

_____

Write down one or two areas of your life in which you have a need or a desire for God to do a work.

1. _____

_____

2. _____

_____

Seek God on the authority of His Word for the answers you need.

Follow the example of David and the royal official concerning these situations in your life. Find two or three promises in God's Word that cover your need or desire, and write them in the space provided. Use your concordance or a Bible promise book if you need help finding a promise from God's Word.

Situation #1:

a. _____

_____

b. _____

_____

c. _____

_____

Situation #2:

a. _____

_____

b. _____

_____

c. _____

_____

Now put your hope in God's promises!

Lesson 2

How Can You Receive God's Great and Precious Promises?

PURPOSE

To realize that all of God's promises belong to you because of Jesus, and to gain a greater understanding of how to receive them in your life.

OVERVIEW

Now that you know God has given you many wonderful promises so you can live an abundant life, you must learn how to receive them. You must establish the fact that because you are a child of God these promises do rightfully belong to you. The Bible teaches that for you to receive all that God has planned, you must add faith and patience to the promises found in His Word. Just as it's important to learn how to receive, it's also important to know what can keep you from receiving God's will for your life. As you study, you'll see that unbelief and lack of knowledge have kept many of God's people from receiving all He has provided for them in Christ Jesus.

DISCUSSION

I. Through Christ Jesus you have been made an heir to every promise found in God's Word.

Read Galatians 3:16, 29: *16The promises were spoken to Abraham and to his seed. The Scripture does not say "and to seeds," meaning many people, but "and to your seed," meaning one person, who is Christ. 29If you belong to Christ, then you are Abraham's seed, and heirs according to the promise.* (NIV)

According to verse 16, to whom did God give His promises?_____

_____

Look at verse 29. Why are you an heir to the promises of God? Why do God's promises belong to you?_____

_____

In Genesis 12:2-3, God promised Abraham that He would bless him, and that all the families of the earth would be blessed through him. In Deuteronomy 28:1-13, God promised Abraham's descendants that He would bless every area of their lives if they would choose to obey Him and walk in His ways. Before Jesus came and died for your sins, you had no rights to the promises God had given Abraham and his descendants (the Jews). Now through the shed blood of Jesus, you've become a seed of Abraham and an heir to every promise God has made in His Word. God's promises are precious because of the price that Jesus paid so that you could receive them in your life. Galatians 3:29 clearly reveals that if you belong to Christ, then every promise God made to Abraham and his seed now belongs to you.

This truth is again stated in Ephesians 2:11-14, 19: *11Therefore remember that at one time you were Gentiles [heathen] in the flesh; called Uncircumcision by those who called themselves Circumcision, [itself a mere mark] in the flesh made by human hands. 12Remember that you were at that time separated (living apart) from Christ — excluded from all part in Him; utterly estranged and outlawed from the rights of Israel as a nation, and strangers with no share in the sacred compacts of the [Messianic] promise — with no knowledge of or right in God's agreements, His covenants. And you had no hope — no promise; you were in the world without God. 13But now in Christ Jesus, you who once were [so] far away, through (by, in) the blood of Christ have been brought near. 14For He is [Himself] our peace — our bond of unity and harmony. He has made us both [Jew and Gentile] one (body), and has broken down (destroyed, abolished) the hostile dividing wall between us.... 19Therefore you are no longer outsiders — exiles, migrants and aliens, excluded from the rights of citizens; but you now share citizenship with the saints — God's own people, consecrated and set apart for Himself; and you belong to God's [own] household.* (AMP)

According to what verse 12 says, then, explain your rights to the promises of God before Jesus shed His blood for you. How were you different from the Jews?_____

_____

_____

_____

Through the blood of Jesus, how has your relationship to God changed? Do you now have a right to the same covenants and promises that God made to Abraham and to his descendants? Why? (Verses 13, 19)_____

_____

_____

The Bible says that all of God's promises are "yes" and "amen" to those who are in Christ Jesus. II Corinthians 1:19-20 says: *19For the Son of God, Jesus Christ, who was preached among you by me and Silas and Timothy, was not "Yes" and "No," but in him it has always been "Yes." 20For no matter how many promises God has made, they are "Yes" in Christ. And so through him the "Amen" is spoken by us to the glory of God.* (NIV)

These verses reveal three very important truths concerning God's promises:

1. God doesn't say "yes" and "no" concerning the promises He has made. His answer is always "yes" in Christ Jesus.

2. Because God's answer is always "yes," you can boldly say, "Amen, so be it in my life." Through Christ Jesus the "amen" is spoken by us. (The second part of this scripture reveals your part in receiving God's promises.)

3. God receives the glory when you partake of His promises.

Now let's examine II Corinthians 1:20 closer, to further grasp the significance of the words "yes" and "amen." To do this, we'll break the scripture into three parts.

Part 1:

II Corinthians 1:20: *For as many as are the promises of God, they all find their Yes (answer) in Him (Christ).* (AMP)

In His Word God has given His people many promises. What has He promised in each of these scriptures?

John 3:16 _____

I John 1:9 _____

Proverbs 4:20-22 _____

I John 5:14-15 _____

Psalm 91:9-11 _____

II Corinthians 9:6-8 _____

Joshua 1:8 _____

Psalm 34:17-19 _____

Philippians 4:6-7 _____

James 1:5 _____

Psalm 37:4 _____

Proverbs 3:5-6 _____

In II Corinthians 1:20, what truth has God revealed to you concerning these promises?

_____

_____

_____

According to II Corinthians 1:19-20, if you belong to Christ, will God's answer to you ever be "no" concerning His promises? Why? _____

_____

Many of God's people have believed that when a person asks God for something in prayer, sometimes His answer is "yes," and sometimes His answer is "no." But, II Corinthians 1:19-20 clearly teaches that if you're in Christ Jesus, God's answer to you concerning His promises is always the divine "yes." If your prayer is based on a promise God has made in His Word, then His answer is always "yes" in Christ. In these verses God has revealed that it's always His will for you to receive His promises. Because of this fact, you can confidently put your trust in every promise God has made in His Word.

When you became a child of God through your faith in Jesus Christ, all of God's promises became available to you. He made you an heir to all the promises found in His Word (Galatians 3:29).

Look back over the list of God's promises. What are some of the many promises that He has given you in His Word?_____

_____

_____

According to II Corinthians 1:20, do these promises belong to you? Is it God's will for you to receive them in your life? What is God's answer?_____

_____

If God declares that His promises are always "yes" in Christ, then why do some of His people fail to receive them in their lives? Let's examine the second part of II Corinthians 1:20 to discover the answer.

Part 2:

II Corinthians 1:20: *For this reason we also utter the Amen (so be it) to God through Him.* (AMP)

God's part:	**Our part:**
• His answer is "yes" in Christ.	• Through Christ Jesus, we utter the "amen" (So be it!).

This section of the verse reveals your part in receiving God's promises. It shows how you should respond to God's Word. When you're convinced that God's answer is always "yes," and when you're confident that His promises belong to you in Christ, you will confidently say "amen" to the promises of God — declaring them to be so in your life.

What does it mean to say "amen" in response to God's promises?

Amen means:

- so be it
- may it become true
- Amen is said after a statement with which one agrees.

When you respond to God's promises by saying "Amen, so be it," you're saying:

- I **agree** with the truth of God's Word!
- May God's promises come true in my life.
- If God promised it, then it belongs to me. I **claim** it to be so in my life.

God's people have a part to play in receiving all that He has provided for them. Although His answer is "yes," His promises won't automatically come to pass in your life. You must respond to what He has promised by putting your absolute trust in His Word. When you speak the "amen" in response to a promise of God, you confirm your faith in His Word.

To gain a clearer understanding of your part in receiving God's promises, let's use the promise of salvation as an example:

God has made His promise of eternal life available to everyone. According to II Corinthians 1:20 His answer is "yes!" He will give you eternal life in Christ Jesus. But, the Bible teaches that until you believe that promise with your heart and confess your faith with your mouth (speak the "amen"), you won't receive the eternal life God has provided for you.

Examine this truth in Romans 10:10: *For with the heart a person believes...* {God's promise} *and with the mouth he confesses — **declares openly and speaks out freely his faith** — and confirms [his] salvation .* {God's promise} (AMP)

What two things does God's Word instruct you to do in order to receive His promise of salvation?

1. _____

2. _____

This scripture reveals that you must believe in your heart and confess your faith with your mouth in order to receive God's promise of salvation. You receive all of God's promises in this same way. When God gives you a promise, you must believe in your heart that His Word is true, and then declare openly and speak out freely about your faith in God's promise. When you boldly confess your faith in His Word, you confirm God's promise to be so in your life. Thus, you've responded by saying, "Amen, so be it in my life!"

According to II Corinthians 1:20, what's your part in receiving God's promises? How must you respond to what He has promised in His Word?_____

_____

Romans 10:10 teaches two ways that you must respond to God's Word in order to receive what He has promised:

1. Believe God's promise with your heart.
2. Confess it to be true with your mouth.

But God's people respond to His promises in other ways, too. Let's examine three of them:

1. Some of God's people reason His promises away because of other people's experiences.

   Example: In Proverbs 22:6, God's Word gives a promise concerning our children: *Train up a child in the way he should go: and when he is old, he will not depart from it.* (KJV)

   The person who reasons God's promises away will read this verse and decide that because there are many good Christian people whose children have departed from God, this scripture must not mean what it says. So, because they don't believe God's promise with their heart, they can't confidently say, "Amen, so be it in my life!" They base their faith on other people's experiences rather than on the truth of God's Word.

2. Some of God's people say they believe what the Bible says is true, but they don't act upon God's Word, nor do they boldly claim His promises to be true in their life. They don't respond to God's "yes" answer by confidently declaring, "Amen, so be it in my life!"

3. Some of God's people put their complete trust in every promise He has made in His Word. They realize that all of His promises belong to them through Christ Jesus; thus, they act upon God's Word and speak in agreement with every word He has spoken. They claim His promises to be true in their life.

These persons boldly agree with God's promise in Proverbs 22:6 by saying, "I'll train my children to follow God, and when they're grown, they won't depart from it."

They believe in their hearts that God's promise is true. They declare openly and speak out freely about their faith. They have confidence that their children won't depart from God because they have a written guarantee in God's Word.

Which type of Christian partakes of God's promises?_____

_____

How have you responded to God's promises? Which type of Christian have you been?

_____

The Bible teaches in Amos 3:3 that if you want to walk with God, you must agree with Him. A person who says "amen" in response to what God has promised is speaking in agreement with Him. When you truly believe God's promise in your heart, you'll boldly confess with your mouth that it's true. Remember, you speak the "amen."

Begin to say "amen" to God's promises by confessing them to be true in your life:

- I have eternal life in Christ Jesus. (John 3:16)
- By the stripes of Jesus I am healed. (I Peter 2: 24)
- My children shall be mighty and blessed upon the earth. (Psalms 112:1-2)
- My God shall supply all my needs. (Philippians 4:19)
- I can do all things through Christ who strengthens me. (Philippians 4:13)
- God has given His angels charge over me to protect me in all my ways. (Psalm 91:9-11)

Have you been boldly declaring God's promises to be true in your life? Have you confirmed your faith in His promises by confessing what you believe?

Part 3:

II Corinthians 1:20: *For no matter how many promises God has made, they are "Yes" in Christ. And so through him the "Amen" is spoken by us to the glory of God.* (NIV)

What does this verse say glorifies God?_____

_____

This section of the verse tells us that God receives the glory when we partake of His promises. God doesn't receive glory when His children experience sickness, lack, discouragement, depression, failure, fear, defeat or tragedy. You should never accept these circumstances as His will for your life, because they go contrary to what His Word teaches. God receives glory when His children partake of all that He has promised: life, health, abundance, success, victory, joy and peace. If you want your life to glorify God, then be a living testimony that He is upright and faithful to the promises He has made in His Word.

II. Examine the characteristics of a person who will inherit the promises of God.

Read Hebrews 6:12. *That ye be not slothful, but followers of them who, through **faith** and **patience**, inherit the promises.* (KJV)

What characteristics must be present in your life for you to inherit the great and precious promises God has given you in His Word? Whose example must you follow?

_____

_____

Verse 12 describes two different types of Christians. Explain the difference between the two.

_____

_____

The Amplified Bible describes a slothful Christian as one who's disinterested in God's Word — a spiritual sluggard — the type of Christian who doesn't diligently seek God.

Two qualities are found in those who will inherit God's promises:

　　　　　　　1.　Faith　　　　　　　　　　　2.　Patience

According to *Strong's Concordance*, the English word "faith" comes from the Greek words *pistis* and *peitho*. Use the definition of these words to gain a clear understanding of faith.

Faith means:
- a conviction of the truthfulness of God
- constancy in such profession — (this definition of faith means a consistent act of openly declaring or publicly proclaiming a belief)
- have confidence
- obey

What does it mean to add faith to God's promises? According to the definition, when you really put your faith in the promises of God, you'll consistently declare them to be true in your life. You'll speak what you believe.

Real faith is made complete by obedience. When you add real faith to God's Word, you'll meet the conditions of His promises. If you truly believe His promise, you'll be obedient to His Word. We'll examine this aspect of faith more closely in Lesson 9.

II Corinthians 4:13 also reveals what it means to add real faith to God's promises: *It is written: "I believed; therefore I have spoken." With that same spirit of faith we also believe and therefore speak.* (NIV)

According to this scripture, what is "the spirit of faith"? What two actions will you take when you add real faith to God's promises?

1. _____
2. _____

Believing with your heart + confessing with your mouth = FAITH

Mark 11: 22-23 once again establishes the truth that when you put your faith in God, you'll boldly speak out about your faith in His promises: *22And Jesus answering saith unto them, Have faith in God. 23For verily I say unto you, That whosoever shall **say** unto this mountain, Be thou removed, and be thou cast into the sea; and shall not doubt in his heart, but shall believe that those things which he **saith** shall come to pass; he shall have whatsoever he **saith**.* (KJV)

According to verse 23, what did Jesus tell you to do to confirm your faith in God?

_____

_____

In this passage of scripture, Jesus explains what it means to have faith in God. He tells you to speak to the mountain. The mountain is the trial or problem that you're facing. It could be sickness, financial struggles, marriage problems, etc. Jesus promises that if you'll speak God's Word to your mountain and not doubt, but believe that what you're saying will happen; then the Word of God which you have spoken will come to pass in your life.

Example: Your mountain may be a financial problem. Your answer can be found in Philippians 4:19, II Corinthians 9:6-11, and Deuteronomy 28:1-13.

If you follow the instructions of Jesus, you'll put your faith in God by speaking His Word to your mountain: "My God shall supply all of my needs. God is able to make all grace abound toward me so that I'll have everything I need in abundance and am able to give to every good work. I'm blessed when I come in and I'm blessed when I go out. God shall bless the works of my hands and I'll be the head and not the tail, above only and not beneath, the lender and not the borrower, for the Word of God has spoken it. Amen, so be it in my life!"

According to Mark 11:23, when you speak God's Word over your situation, and firmly believe that it will come to pass in your life, then you've put your faith in God.

Now that we've established what it means to add faith to God's Word, remember, you must add patience to your faith.

Patience means:

- endurance through any trial
- the quality that refuses to give up
- the quality that does not surrender to circumstances or give up under trial
- perseverance and persistence

Many times God's people don't have the quality that refuses to give up. They receive God's promises with excitement; but if they don't see their circumstances begin to change quickly, they give up. You must be determined to receive all that God has provided for you in every area of your life: your marriage, your children, your finances and your health. Don't settle for second best or what you can endure. Go for God's best! Be determined to receive everything that Jesus paid the price for you to have. Take an attitude that refuses to give up, and persevere until you receive the promise.

Although God wants His people to partake of His promises, many Christians don't receive all that He wants for them.

III. The Bible describes two reasons why some of God's people fail to receive His promises.

Read Hosea 4:6: *My people are destroyed for lack of knowledge, because thou hast rejected knowledge.* (KJV)

Write one reason why some of God's people fail to receive His promises.

_____

Notice, this scripture is talking about God's people. It doesn't say unbelievers are destroyed for lack of knowledge; it says God's people are destroyed because they lack knowledge of His Word. This verse also reveals that some of God's people don't receive victory in their lives because they reject the knowledge of His Word. They refuse to believe that His promises are true.

If you want to receive all the wonderful promises God has given you in His Word, you must know what He has provided for you in Christ Jesus. Lacking knowledge or rejecting knowledge will keep you from partaking of His perfect will for your life. Through Christ you're an heir to all of God's promises. His Word is His written will for you; it's the inheritance that you have received as His child.

For example: Before people die, they write a will in order to leave an inheritance for their children. If the children never read the will to discover what they've inherited, they'll never know what belongs to them. And if they don't take the proper steps to claim their inheritance, they'll never receive what their parents provided for them.

In the same way, the Bible is God's will for you because you're His child. He sent Jesus to die for you so that you can receive your inheritance. You must take the time to search God's Word and discover what you've inherited so you'll know what rightfully belongs to you. You must take the proper steps to receive your inheritance or you'll never partake of what your Heavenly Father has provided.

Acts 20:32 says *I commend you to the Word of His grace — to the commands and counsels and promises of His unmerited favor. It is able to build you up and to give you [your rightful] inheritance among all God's set-apart ones — those consecrated, purified and transformed of soul.* (AMP)

What is God's Word able to do?

_____

God's Word consists of His commands, His counsel and His promises. When you grow in the knowledge of God's Word and apply it to your life, it's able to strengthen you and give you your rightful inheritance, which includes all of God's promises.

Hebrews 4:1-2 offers another reason some of God's people fail to receive His promises: *1Therefore, while the promise of entering His rest still holds and is offered [today], let us be afraid [to distrust it], lest any of you should think he has come too late and has come short of [reaching] it. 2For indeed we have had the glad tidings [of God] proclaimed to us just as truly as they [the Israelites of old did when the good news of deliverance from bondage came to them]; but the message they heard did not benefit them, **because it was not mixed with faith**.* (AMP)

God's people had knowledge of what He had promised them, yet it didn't benefit their lives. Why? (verse 2)_____

_____

In Numbers 13:1-2, God promised His people deliverance from bondage. He promised them a land flowing with milk and honey, a place where they would overflow in His blessings. But God's people didn't combine faith with His promise. Unbelief kept them from receiving the fulfillment of what God had promised them. Of all the children of Israel to whom God had given His promise, only two received what He had planned. Joshua and Caleb entered the land of Canaan because they added their faith to God's Word. They believed His promise with their hearts and boldly confessed it to be true. Everyone else reasoned it away — and died in the wilderness as a result. (Numbers 13:17-14:29)

So you see, even though God gives you a promise, the way you respond to it determines whether or not you will receive it. God has given you many promises, just as He did the children of Israel; but you must be careful not to follow the example of the Israelites. They didn't add faith and patience to God's Word; thus, they didn't partake of what He had promised them. If you want to experience all God has promised you, you must follow the example of Joshua and Caleb and confirm your faith by boldly declaring His promises to be true in your life.

SUMMARY

All of God's promises have become available to you through the shed blood of Jesus. When you ask God to fulfill His promises in your life, His answer will always be "yes" in Christ. You must respond to His promises by putting your absolute trust in His Word. You must say, "Amen, so be it in my life!" A lack of knowledge, and unbelief have kept some of God's people from receiving what He has provided for them. God's people who add real faith to His promises will boldly confess them to be true. And because of this, they'll partake of the wonderful plan that God has for their life.

PERSONAL APPLICATION

If you want to live a victorious Christian life, you must spend time meditating on God's Word. Memorize and meditate on the scriptures you studied in this lesson. Read Psalm 1:1-3.

Memorize and meditate on the following verses:

Galatians 3:29: *If you belong to Christ, then you are Abraham's seed, and heirs according to the promise.* (NIV)

II Corinthians 1:20: *No matter how many promises God has made, they are "Yes" in Christ. And so through Him the "Amen" is spoken by us to the glory of God.* (NIV)

Hebrews 6:12: *Be not slothful, but followers of them who through faith and patience inherit the promises.* (KJV)

II Corinthians 4:13: *It is written: "I believed; therefore I have spoken." With that same spirit of faith we also believe and therefore speak.* (NIV)

Recall the promises that you wrote down in the Personal Application in Lesson 1.

Situation #1:

a. _____

b. _____

c. _____

Situation #2:

a. _____

b. _____

c. _____

REVIEW QUESTIONS

1. Why do God's promises belong to you? (Galatians 3:29)_____
   _____

2. Explain the truth revealed in II Corinthians 1:20 concerning God's promises. What is your part in receiving these promises from God in your life?_____
   _____
   _____

3. How can you inherit these promises of God? (Hebrews 6:12) _____
   _____

4. What are the two parts to faith? When you add real faith to God's promises, what two actions will you take? (II Corinthians 4:13)_____
   _____

5. What promise did God give you in Mark 11:23?_____
   _____

6. What does it mean to add patience to your faith? Describe the quality found in patience.
   _____
   _____

7. What two things will keep you from receiving the promises of God in your life?
   _____
   _____

Remember, if you truly believe that God will perform His promises in your life, then you'll boldly confess and openly speak about your faith in His promises. God's answer to these promises is **"Yes" in Christ Jesus**. Respond to God's Word by saying, **"Amen, so be it in my life!"** If you'll speak God's Word to your mountain, and do not doubt in your heart, God will perform His promises in your life. You have a written guarantee in His Word (Mark 11:22-24).

Lesson 3
God Is Faithful to His Promises

PURPOSE

To gain a greater understanding of your Heavenly Father's faithfulness. When you realize that He won't fail to keep His promises, you'll put your complete confidence in Him.

OVERVIEW

In the previous lesson you learned that lack of knowledge will keep you from receiving God's will for your life. Many times God's people lack knowledge of the character of their Heavenly Father. They don't have a full understanding of His faithfulness, so they struggle to put their trust in His promises. As you renew your mind to the scriptures in this lesson, you'll realize that God's Word is trustworthy. When you understand that your Heavenly Father won't allow His Word to fail, you'll be able to put your trust in Him and receive all that He has promised.

DISCUSSION

I. God is faithful to His Word.

You must be convinced that God is faithful to His Word before you can really trust in what He has promised.

In Hebrews 11:11 you can see an example of a person who was confident of God's faithfulness. *Because of faith also Sarah herself received physical power to conceive a child, even when she was long past the age for it, because she considered [God] Who had given her the promise to be reliable and trustworthy and true to His Word.* (AMP)

Even though what God had promised Sarah seemed impossible in the natural, she was able to put her trust in His promise. Why?_____

_____

_____

Sarah received God's promise because she believed His Word. She was able to look past her present circumstances and put her trust in His promise because she considered His faithfulness. She was convinced that He would remain true to His Word. Even though God's promise was impossible in the natural, Sarah was confident that He was able to perform what He had promised her. As you seek God's Word, you'll discover many wonderful promises that He has made to you, His child. Many times, however, His promises seem too good to be true. They seem impossible in the natural, so we allow our circumstances to cause us to doubt His Word. In order to be able to trust in what God has promised, you must be convinced, just as Sarah was, that He is trustworthy and faithful to His Word.

Only through God's Word are you able to know the character of your Heavenly Father.

Read I Corinthians 1:9. *God is faithful (reliable, trustworthy, and therefore ever true to His promise, and He can be depended on).* (AMP)

Read Psalm 145:13. *The Lord is faithful to all his promises.* (NIV)

What do these scriptures reveal about God's character? _____

_____

God is faithful to the promises He has given you in His Word. Because of His faithfulness, His Word can be fully trusted and is worthy of complete confidence.

Psalms 138:2 contains a powerful truth concerning God's Word: *I will worship toward Your holy temple, and praise Your name for Your loving-kindness and for Your truth and faithfulness; for You have exalted above all else Your name and Your word and You have magnified Your word above all Your name!* (AMP)

What has God magnified above His very name?_____

_____

Does this truth enable you to place even more confidence in the promises of God's Word? Explain._____

_____

_____

The Bible is the inspired Word of God (II Timothy 3:16). God spoke through men so you can know Him and His will for you. I Thessalonians 2:13 says that His people are to accept the scriptures *not as the word of [mere] men, but as what it truly is, the Word of God.* God so wants you to be able to trust in His Word with such confidence that He has magnified it above His very name.

In *The Living Bible,* Psalm 138:2 states: *I face your Temple as I worship, giving thanks to you for all your lovingkindness and your faithfulness, for your promises are backed by all the honor of your name.*

What truth is revealed in this scripture concerning God's promises?

_____

_____

_____

A promise is only as good as the person who makes it; people are known by what they do. Thus, if a person makes promises and then fails to keep them, he can't be trusted — his name can't be trusted. God's name can be trusted because He's faithful to His promises.

God has given many promises to those who will trust Him. Some of His promises include:

- healing (James 5:14-16)
- financial abundance (Deuteronomy 8:18)
- peace (Phillipians 4:6-7)
- righteousness (Romans 3:21-22)
- guidance (Proverbs 3:5-6)

- eternal life (John 3:16)
- victory (I John 5:4)
- success (Joshua 1:8)
- protection (Psalm 91)
- answered prayer (I John 5:14-15)

Because God wants you to be able to trust in His promises with great confidence, He has backed them with all the honor of His name. Looking up the meaning of the word "honor" in a dictionary, we learn that a man of honor always keeps his promises.

Because God wants you to be totally convinced of the integrity of His Word, He has exalted it above His very name. If His Word fails, then He Himself fails. However, the Bible teaches that it's impossible for Him to prove false and lie to His people. He will be faithful to perform what He has promised.

Read Hebrews 6:13-18: *13When God made his promise to Abraham, since there was no one greater for him to swear by, he swore by himself, 14 saying, "I will surely bless you and give you many descendants." 15And so after waiting patiently, Abraham received what was promised. 16Men swear by someone greater than themselves, and the oath confirms what is said and puts an end to all argument. 17Because God wanted to make the unchanging nature of his purpose very clear to the heirs of what was promised, he confirmed it with an oath. 18God did this so that, by two unchangeable things in which it is impossible for God to lie, we who have fled to take hold of the hope offered to us may be greatly encouraged.* (NIV)

Why has God confirmed His promises with an oath? (verse 17)_____
_____
_____

What is it impossible for God to do? (verse 18)_____
_____

Why do you have a guarantee that God won't fail to keep His promises? Why can you be greatly encouraged? (verses 17-18)_____
_____
_____

In *The Living Bible* Hebrews 6:17-18 states: *17God also bound himself with an oath, so that those he promised to help would be perfectly sure and never need to wonder whether he might change his plans. 18He has given us both his promise and his oath, two things we can completely count on, for it is impossible for God to tell a lie.*

Why can you be perfectly sure and confident that God will keep His promises? (verse 17)
_____
_____
_____

Look at verse 18. What two things can you completely count on? Why?_____

_____

_____

You can see this truth again in Numbers 23:19: *God is not a man, that he should lie, nor a son of man, that he should change his mind. Does he speak and then not act? Does he promise and not fulfill?* (NIV)

How does this scripture reaffirm to you that God will keep His promises? _____

_____

_____

Psalm 89:33-34 also establishes the fact that God won't allow His promises to fail or prove false: *33Nevertheless, My loving-kindness will I not break off from him, nor allow My faithfulness to fail [to lie and be false to him]. 34My covenant will I not break or profane, nor alter the thing that is gone out of my lips.* (AMP)

What does God say He will never allow? How does this truth strengthen your trust in His Word?_____

_____

_____

Will God ever break His covenant with you? Will He ever change His mind concerning His promises?

You learned in II Corinthians 1:19-20 that God doesn't say "yes" and "no" concerning His promises. He will never change His mind. Because of Jesus, His answer to you concerning His promises is always "yes!"

In Ezekiel 12:25 God confirms that He will be faithful to perform what He has spoken in His Word: *For I am the Lord; I will speak, and the word that I shall speak shall be performed (come to pass); it shall be no more delayed or prolonged, for in your days, O rebellious house, I will speak the word and will perform it, says the Lord God.* (AMP)

You can see this truth again in Jeremiah 1:12: *Then said the Lord to me, You have seen well, for I am alert and active, watching over My word to perform it.* (AMP)

What has God strongly stated in both of these scriptures? How does this build your confidence in His Word?_____

_____

_____

God clearly shows in these scriptures that if He has promised something in His Word, He will bring it to pass. You can claim His promises with confidence because He is alert and active, watching over His Word to perform it. God won't lie or deceive you. His Word is completely trustworthy. When you put your complete trust in His promises, you can be confident that He will make sure they come to pass in your life.

If you'll put your trust in the following promises, what will God perform in your life?

Psalm 37:4 _____

Psalm 103:2-3 _____

Psalm 91:9-11 _____

Remember, God watches over His Word to perform it!

Psalm 12: 6-7 says, *6The words and promises of the Lord are pure words, like silver refined in an earthen furnace, purified seven times over. 7You will keep them and preserve them, O Lord.* (AMP)

Now that you realize God will always be faithful to fulfill His promises, look at how you can confidently respond to His Word.

Read Hebrews 10:23: *So let us seize and hold fast and retain without wavering the hope we cherish and confess and our acknowledgment of it, for He Who promised is reliable (sure) and faithful to His word.* (AMP)

What five actions does this scripture tell you to take concerning your hope in God's promises?

1. _____
2. _____
3. _____
4. _____
5. _____

Take a closer look at the definition of each of these words to get a clearer understanding of how you should respond to God's promises.

1. *seize*: to take possession of
2. *hold fast*: grasp firmly (Don't let go!)
3. *retain without wavering*: to keep in mind without hesitating or doubting
4. *confess*: to declare openly and speak out freely about (your faith in God's promise)
5. *acknowledgment of it*: act of admitting that something is true

In which of God's promises have you put your hope concerning a specific need or desire?

_____

_____

_____

According to the definitions of the previous words, explain the five actions that God wants you to take concerning these promises.

1. _____
2. _____
3. _____

4. _____

5. _____

According to Hebrews 10:23, why can you confess with confidence that God will fulfill these promises in your life?_____

_____

You can hold on to God's promises without hesitating or doubting, and you can confidently confess them to be true in your life because God, Who has given you these promises, is reliable and trustworthy and faithful to His Word.

II. Those who trust God will experience His faithfulness.

Read Psalm 37:3: *Trust (lean on, rely on, and be confident) in the Lord and do good; so shall you dwell in the land and feed surely on His faithfulness, and truly you shall be fed.* (AMP)

What must you do to feed upon God's faithfulness? To whom is God faithful?

_____

_____

Those who trust in the Lord (those who rely on, lean on, and put their confidence in God's Word) will feed upon His faithfulness, and will be completely satisfied.

Read James 1:6-7. *6But when he asks, he must believe and not doubt, because he who doubts is like a wave of the sea, blown and tossed by the wind. 7That man should not think he will receive anything from the Lord.* (NIV)

Will those who doubt God's Word experience His faithfulness? Explain the truth revealed in this scripture. _____

_____

_____

Nahum 1:7 says *the Lord is good, a Strength and Stronghold in the day of trouble; He knows (recognizes, has knowledge of, and understands) those who take refuge and trust in Him.* (AMP) II Chronicles 16:9 says *the eyes of the Lord run to and fro throughout the whole earth to show Himself strong in behalf of those whose hearts are blameless toward Him.* (AMP) God knows when you're completely trusting Him. When you completely trust Him, He will do a powerful work in your life.

Your heart is blameless before God when you choose to put your trust in Him. Hebrews 11:6 teaches that without faith it's impossible to please God. When you put your complete trust in His Word, you'll boldly confess His promises to be true in your life. You've already learned that the spirit of faith is characterized by believing in your heart and confessing with your mouth. This is the kind of faith that pleases God.

Read Deuteronomy 7:9: *Know, recognize, and understand therefore that the Lord your God, He is God, the faithful God, Who keeps covenant and steadfast love and mercy with those who love Him and keep His commandments, to a thousand generations.* (AMP)

What does God want you to know and understand?_____

_____

_____

With whom is God faithful to keep His promises?_____

_____

Read I John 3:22-23: *And whatsoever we ask, we receive from him, because we keep his commandments, and do those things that are pleasing in his sight. And this is his commandment, that we should believe on the name of his son Jesus Christ, and love one another, as he gave us commandment.* (KJV)

When is God faithful to answer your prayers? What commandments did He give you?

_____

_____

Two characteristics are evident in the lives of those who experience the faithfulness of God:

      1. Trust (Psalm 37:3)   2. Obedience (Deuteronomy 7:9)

Psalm 22:4-5 teaches us that those who trust God will never be ashamed, confused, or disappointed. *4Our fathers trusted in You; they trusted (leaned on, relied on You, and were confident) and You delivered them. 5They cried to You and were delivered; they trusted in, leaned on, and confidently relied on You, and were not ashamed or confounded or disappointed.* (AMP)

Has God ever failed anyone who has put their complete confidence in Him? What truth is revealed in this scripture? _____

_____

_____

This truth is again shown in Romans 9:33. *As it is written, Behold I am laying in Zion a Stone that will make men stumble, a Rock that will make them fall; but he who believes in Him [who adheres to, trusts in, and relies on Him] shall not be put to shame nor be disappointed in his expectations.* (AMP)

Who will never be disappointed in their expectations?_____

_____

_____

Through Christ Jesus you've inherited all of God's promises (II Corinthians 1:20); therefore, because of Jesus, you can confidently expect God to fulfill His promises in your life. When you put your trust in what Jesus has done for you, you'll never be disappointed. When you realize that all of God's promises find their "yes" answer in your life because of Jesus, you'll rest in every promise that God has made in His Word, and you'll experience His faithfulness. When your expectations are based on what God has promised, you'll never be disappointed. God confirms this truth in Isaiah 49:23: *"I am the Lord; those who hope in me will not be disappointed.* (NIV)

What has God promised you if you'll put your hope in His Word?_____

_____

Hebrews 13:5 strongly reemphasizes that God won't fail those who trust Him. *"For He [God] Himself has said, I will not in any way fail you nor give you up nor leave you without support. [I will] not, [I will] not, [I will] not in any degree leave you helpless nor forsake nor let [you] down (relax My hold on you)! [Assuredly not!]"* AMP

What has God promised in this scripture? _____

_____

God is always faithful to His promises. If you'll put your trust in His Word, you'll never be disappointed. However, many of God's people have become disappointed simply because they've tried to trust God to do something that He didn't promise He would do. For example, God didn't promise He would answer your prayer according to your schedule.

Putting a deadline on when you expect God to fulfill His promise, often leads to disappointment. God says that through faith and patience you'll inherit His promises (Hebrews 6:12). Putting a time limit on something you're expecting God to do eliminates the need for patience. Patience is what keeps you from becoming disappointed when you face circumstances contrary to what God has promised you; it's perseverance and persistence. It doesn't surrender to circumstances. It produces an attitude that says, "I won't give up until the answer comes." If you'll be patient, you'll never be disappointed in your expectations. (Read Hebrews 6:15.)

Have you ever been disappointed by putting a time limit on God? Explain.

_____

_____

Setting your eyes on a specific way that you want God to fulfill His promise also often leads to disappointment. God knows what's best for you. You must trust that His ways are perfect. For example, if you're trusting God for a better job to provide for your family and you set your eyes on a specific job, you'll probably be disappointed if that very job doesn't come through. On the other hand, if you keep your eyes on God's promise to direct and prosper you, you can be confident that He has the right job in store for you and you won't be disappointed. God will open a door of opportunity if you'll put your confidence in Him. You mustn't set your eyes on a particular way that you want God to answer your prayer.

Isaiah 55:8-9 says: *"For my thoughts are not your thoughts, neither are your ways my ways,"* declares the Lord. *"As the heavens are higher than the earth, so are my ways higher than your ways and my thoughts than your thoughts."* (NIV) In other words, the way God accomplishes something won't always be your way. The way you figure something out won't always be the way that God has it figured out. Therefore, if you'll focus on God's promise and leave the how and when up to Him, you'll never be disappointed. God is always faithful to those who put their trust in His promises. You must trust that God's ways and His timing are perfect.

Have you been disappointed by getting your eyes on a specific way that you wanted God to fulfill His promise? Explain._____

_____

Recall the promises that you put your hope in for your specific situation. What two things must you avoid to keep from being disappointed in your expectations?

1. _____

2. _____

Read Psalm 92:12, 14-15: 12*The [uncompromisingly] righteous shall flourish like the palm tree [be long-lived, stately, upright, useful, and fruitful]; they shall grow like a cedar in Lebanon [majestic, stable, durable, and incorruptible]....14[Growing in grace] they shall still bring forth fruit in old age; they shall be full of sap [of spiritual vitality] and [rich in the] verdure [of trust, love, and contentment]. 15[They are living memorials] to show that the Lord is upright and faithful to His promises; He is my Rock, and there is no unrighteousness in Him.* (AMP)

Describe, according to verse 14, the spiritual strengths of the uncompromising righteous.

_____

_____

_____

What do their lives prove about God?(verse 15)_____

_____

If you'll trust and obey God's Word, people will look at your life and see His blessings. You'll be a living testimony to show that God is upright and faithful to His promises. Your life will glorify God because you'll testify of His faithfulness.

SUMMARY

God is faithful. He's trustworthy and true to His promises. You can be confident that God will always keep His promises because He has backed them with all the honor of His name. If you'll put your absolute trust in His Word, you'll feed upon His faithfulness. Those who doubt God's Word can't expect to receive anything from Him. Whatever the situation you're facing, find a promise in God's Word and confidently confess it to be true in your life. You'll be a living testimony that God is faithful to His promises.

PERSONAL APPLICATION

This week take time to renew your mind to God's faithfulness. Meditate on the following scriptures:

First Corinthians 1:9 *God is faithful (reliable, trustworthy, and therefore ever true to His promise, and He can be depended on).* (AMP)

Jeremiah 1:12: *Then said the Lord to me, You have seen well, for I am alert and active, watching over My word to perform it.* (AMP)

Hebrews 10:23: *So let us seize and hold fast and retain without wavering the hope we cherish and confess and our acknowledgment of it, for He Who promised is reliable (sure) and faithful to His word.* (AMP)

Psalm 37:3: *Trust (lean on, rely on, and be confident) in the Lord and do good; so shall you dwell in the land and feed surely on His faithfulness.* (AMP)

REVIEW QUESTIONS

1. What must you understand about God's character in order to really put your trust in Him?_____
_____

2. What two characteristics must be present in your life in order to experience God's faithfulness? (Psalm 37:3, Deuteronomy 7:9)_____
_____

3. Who will never be disappointed in their expectations? (Romans 9:33)_____
_____

4. What two things can lead you to disappointment?_____
_____

5. Why are you able to confess with complete confidence that God's promises will come to pass in your life ? (Hebrews 10:23) _____
_____

6. If you put your complete confidence in God's promises, how will your life glorify Him? (Psalm 92:15 AMP) _____
_____

Follow Sarah's example and put your confidence in God's faithfulness. Apply Hebrews 11:11 to your situation by personalizing it and fitting it to your specific situation. (See the following example.)

Because of faith_____ received _____
        (Write in your name,)

_____
_____
_____
        (Write in the promises you've put your hope in and their scripture reference.)

because _____ considered God who had given her/him the promise, to be reliable
        (Write in your name.)
(sure) and faithful to His Word.

Example: Because of faith <u>Mary</u> received <u>guidance for God's will in her life (Proverbs 3:5-6), financial needs met (Philippians 4:19), and healing (James 5:14-16)</u>, because <u>Mary</u> considered God, who had given her the promise, to be reliable (sure) and faithful to His Word.

Lesson 4
God's Promises for Your Marriage and Your Children

PURPOSE

To discover what God has promised concerning your marriage and your children so that you don't lack knowledge of His perfect will for your life.

OVERVIEW

Now that you realize God is trustworthy and faithful, you can begin to study some of the many promises He has made in His Word. You've already learned that through Christ Jesus you are an heir to every promise God has made. However, if you lack knowledge of what God has promised, you won't receive what rightfully belongs to you as a child of God. As you study God's Word, you'll discover His perfect will for your marriage and your children. God has promised that if you pray according to His will, He'll hear and answer your prayers. When you put your absolute trust in this promise, you'll receive the wonderful plan He has for your life.

DISCUSSION

I. God has given you promises for your marriage.

What has God promised the wife concerning her husband?

Read Proverbs 31:10-11, 23, & 28-30.

In these verses God's Word says three things concerning her husband will happen in the life of the virtuous woman. What are they?

1. (verse 11) _____

_____

2. (verse 23)_____

_____

3. (verses 28-29)_____

_____

According to the original Hebrew text, the word translated "known" in verse 23 means "be diligent; have knowledge; have respect; man of skill." According to this scripture, then, if a wife will trust and obey God, He'll do such a work in her husband's life that her husband will be respected for his knowledge and wisdom when he sits among the elders (those who are in authority) in the land. He'll be diligent and skillful in his work and God will cause him to be successful in every area of his life.

The desire of every Christian woman's heart is for her husband to trust and confide in her. She wants him to be successful and respected by others. Every woman has a desire for her husband to love her so much that he thinks she's the greatest of them all. Your Heavenly Father knew you'd have these desires because He's the One Who placed them in your heart. He loves you so much that He promised the very things you desire most for your husband. The Bible wasn't written so you could read Proverbs 31 and say, "How I wish this were true in my life." It was written so that you can have hope in your situation. It was written so you can see what your Heavenly Father wants for you!

God also knows the only way you can receive these desires of your heart is to completely depend on Him. He wants you to realize that it's only by His grace that you can become the virtuous woman He wants you to be. And it's only by the grace of God that your husband can become all that you want him to be. All God requires from you is that you completely trust in Him. He wants you to realize that nothing is impossible if you'll only believe.

Luke 1:37 says, *For with God **nothing is ever impossible** and no word from God shall be without power or impossible of fulfillment.* (AMP)

According to Proverbs 31:11, 23, & 28-29, what is God's will for your husband?

_____

_____

_____

_____

Do you believe that God is able to fulfill these scriptures in your husband's life? Explain.

_____

_____

Does Luke 1:37 give you hope that the scriptures found in Proverbs 31 can become a reality in your life?_____

_____

Proverbs 31 describes God's perfect plan for you. He is able to bring that plan to pass. Nothing is impossible for Him. If you'll put your trust in Him, He'll watch over His Word, found in Proverbs 31, and perform it in your life.

What has God promised the husband concerning His wife?

Read Psalm 128: 1-4.

According to verse 3, what promise, concerning his wife, does God give to the man who fears Him? _____

_____

According to the original Hebrew text, the word translated "fruitful" in this scripture means "to cause to be fruitful, to bring forth fruit." If a man will trust and obey God, God will do a work in his wife causing her to bring forth fruit. She'll become a fruitful vine within his home.

Galatians 5:22-23 gives us an example of the fruit that the Holy Spirit produces: 22*But the fruit of the [Holy] Spirit [the work which His presence within accomplishes] is love, joy (gladness), peace, patience...kindness...goodness...faithfulness...*23*Gentleness...self-control...* (AMP)

If you begin to trust in God to work in your wife's heart, what fruit will develop in her life?
_____

_____

God promises in Psalm 128:3 that if you'll obey Him and trust in His Word, the fruit of the Spirit will become evident in your wife's life.

Proverbs 19:14 says *a wise, understanding and prudent wife is from the Lord.* (AMP) Again, you can see that the fruit that will be present in your wife comes from the Lord. God's grace will change and perfect her into the virtuous woman you want her to be. You must trust God to do a work inside both of you if you want to receive His promises concerning your marriage.

According to Proverbs 31:30 and Psalm 128:1, what characteristic is present in the man and woman who will receive God's promises concerning their spouse?_____

_____

What does it mean to fear the Lord? (Deuteronomy 10:12-13)_____

_____

_____

Read Psalm 34: 11-14. How do these verses describe one who fears the Lord?_____

_____

_____

When you truly walk in the fear of the Lord, you want, above all things, to please God. You'll conform your life to the wisdom and instruction you find in His Word. You'll be committed to becoming the husband or wife He wants you to be.

In His Word, God has revealed His perfect plan for every Christian marriage. When you fully understand God's will, you can conform your life to it and trust Him to bring to pass His perfect plan for your marriage.

Let's look first at God's will for the wife. Describe what the following scriptures say are characteristics found in the virtuous woman. What is God's will for every wife?

Proverbs 31:12 _____

_____

Proverbs 31:26 _____

_____

Proverbs 31:27 _____

_____

I Peter 3:1-2 says, 1*In like manner, you married women, be submissive to your own husbands... so that even if any do not obey the Word [of God], they may be won over not by discussion but by the [godly] lives of their wives,* 2*When they observe the pure and modest way in which you conduct yourselves, together with your reverence [for your husband; you are to feel for him all that reverence includes: to respect, defer to, revere him — to honor, esteem, appreciate, prize, and, in the human sense, to adore him, that is, to admire, praise, be devoted to, deeply love, and enjoy your husband].* (AMP)

According to verse 1, how can a husband who doesn't obey God's Word be won over?

_____

_____

God wants what characteristics to be present in the wife? (verse 2) _____

_____

_____

_____

Describe, according to I Corinthians 13:4-7, the kind of love God wants a woman to have for her husband. To get a clearer understanding of how to apply this in your own life, insert your name or your wife's name in the place of "love" when answering this question.

_____

_____

_____

_____

_____

Read I Timothy 2:1-4 and Ephesians 6:17-18. What does God want the wife to be continually doing for her husband? _____

_____

How will a wife's prayers affect her husband? (James 5:16) _____

_____

Now let's look at God's will for the husband. Describe, according to the following scriptures, the characteristics of the man who fears the Lord. What is God's will for every husband?

Ephesians 5:23 _____

_____

Ephesians 5:25 _____

_____

Ephesians 5:26 _____

_____

As Christ sanctifies and cleanses the Church with His Word, so a husband should sanctify his wife through his kind and loving words.

Describe, according to I Corinthians 13:4-7, the kind of love a man should have for his wife. To get a clearer understanding of how to apply this to your own life, insert your name or your husband's name in the place of "love" when answering this question.

_____

_____

_____

_____

_____

Ephesians 5:28-29 and I Timothy 5:8 _____

_____

Colossians 3:19_____

_____

Now that you understand God's perfect will for your marriage, and you realize His plan for you, you must learn how to trust God to bring His will to pass in your life.

Read I John 5:14-15. This is God's promise to you.

What has He promised in these verses?_____

_____

_____

According to verse 14, when can you have confidence that God will hear when you pray for your marriage?_____

_____

According to the scriptures you've studied, what is God's will for your marriage?

_____

_____

_____

_____

_____

Look at verse 15. When you pray for yourself and your spouse according to the will of God, what can you confidently know? _____

_____

Through His Word, God has shown His will for your marriage. He wants His perfect plan to come to pass in your life. He has promised that if you'll pray for your marriage according to His will, He will hear and listen to your prayers. And if you positively know that God hears you, then you'll also know, with the same confident assurance, that He will bring to pass the answer to your prayer.

When you begin to pray God's Word over your marriage and ask Him to develop His love inside your hearts for one another, His grace begins to change you into the husband and the wife that He created you to be.

Is God really able to change your situation? Can He really change you and your spouse?

First, you must realize that you and your spouse can't become what God wants you to be without completely depending on Him.

Read Romans 7:18. *For I know that nothing good dwells within me, that is, in my flesh. I can will what is right, but I cannot perform it. [I have the intention and urge to do what is right, but no power to carry it out.]* (AMP)

Do you and your spouse have the ability within yourselves to become what God wants you to be? In his own natural ability, can a husband really love his wife with God's kind of love? Can a wife become a virtuous woman through just her own ability? Explain the truth found in this scripture._____

_____

_____

You must understand that without the power and ability of God at work in your lives, it's impossible to have the marriage you desire. This scripture clearly teaches that even though you may want to be the wife or husband that God wants you to be, you have no power to carry it out in the flesh (by your own power). It's impossible for a husband and wife to love one another with God's unconditional love apart from complete dependence on Him.

When God created man, He put within him a need and desire to be loved, admired and respected. So God made woman to meet that need in man. He placed similar human desires in the woman — to be loved and cared for. However, God didn't want man and woman to be completely satisfied with each other, and therefore have no need for Him. So God made it impossible for the man and woman to meet each other's needs apart from complete dependence on Him. In other words, the only love that completely satisfies is God's love. And the only way you can love with God's unconditional love is to trust in Him to develop His love within you. God's kind of love is a love that is patient and kind; a love that is never envious or proud; a love that is unselfish and takes no account of wrongs done to it. God's love in you causes you to see the best in your spouse.

So you see, when you realize that your spouse is incapable in the flesh of loving you the way you want to be loved, it draws you back to God. If you try to change your spouse by nagging and complaining, you'll only become frustrated, for they have no power to change. When you look to your spouse, you become frustrated and irritated if they aren't being what you want them to be. But if you'll look to God and depend on Him, God will create in them the desire and ability to be everything you want them to be. It's only by God's grace that a husband can become the spiritual head of his home and fulfill God's plan for his life. It's only by God's grace that he can love his wife with God's kind of love. And it's only by the grace of God that a wife can become the virtuous woman that her husband wants her to be. When you begin to trust in God, His grace is able to do a powerful work in your marriage.

Read I Corinthians 15:9-10.

What changed Paul's heart? What changed him from a persecutor of the Church into a mighty man of God?_____

What must be at work in your lives in order for you and your spouse to be changed into the husband and wife that God wants you to be?_____

The grace of God working in Paul's life changed his heart and drew him into the kingdom of God. That same grace was at work in him so that he was able to fulfill the plan God had for his life. The Bible teaches that as husband and wife you are joint-heirs to the life-changing power of God's grace.

I Peter 3:7 says, *In the same way you married men should live considerately with [your wives]...[realizing that you] are joint heirs of the grace (God's unmerited favor) of life.* (AMP)

What does God want you to realize?_____

_____

The original Greek word translated "grace" in this scripture means "the divine influence (of God) upon the heart, and its reflection in the life." In other words, the grace of God is His influence upon your hearts which causes change to take place in your lives.

II Corinthians 1:12 gives you a clear understanding of what God's grace does in a person's life: *The grace of God (the unmerited favor and merciful kindness by which God, exerting His holy influence upon souls, turns them to Christ, and keeps, strengthens, and increases them in Christian virtues).* (AMP)

According to this scripture, grace is the divine influence of God upon your spouse's heart, which turns them toward Christ and changes them into the spouse that God wants them to be.

It's important for you to realize that God's grace is His power within a person to bring change. His grace changes people. By God's grace you and your spouse will become what He created you to be. You can receive His life-changing power through faith (Ephesians 2:7-8). When you begin to truly look to God and trust in Him to change your spouse, His power and ability will begin to work in their heart, and it's reflected in their life by their expression of love for you, and their desire to obey God.

How exciting it is when you realize that you are joint-heirs to this life-changing grace of God. You can not only trust in God's grace to change you, but you can also trust in His grace to change your spouse.

James 4:6 says *he gives us more grace. That is why the scripture says: "God opposes the proud but gives grace to the humble."* (NIV)

So often in a marriage relationship we're only concerned about our spouse changing. We think, "if only they would change." But in order to receive the grace of God in your marriage you must first be humble enough to say, "Lord, change me. Create in me the desire and ability to be the spouse you want me to be. Help me to love my spouse with your unconditional love." Then, you must trust in God's ability to change your spouse.

What about your spouse's will?

Deuteronomy 30:15-19 teaches that God has given each of us a choice between obeying or disobeying His Word. Every one of us has to make a decision — to choose to obey or to disobey God. But the Bible also teaches that God has the power to influence a person's will and create in them the desire to obey Him.

The Bible teaches us to rightly divide the Word of truth. It's true that your spouse has a will to choose; and this truth has been emphasized. However, very little emphasis and very little teaching has been given to the truth concerning God's power to influence your spouse's will when you pray for them. In many instances the only truth that has been taught is that each person must choose between obeying or disobeying God. When this is emphasized and the truth concerning the power of God's influence is not, it often produces doubt and discouragement in the heart of those who have been praying for their spouse. Many times it has discouraged them from even praying at all.

The Bible teaches that if one spouse in a marriage relationship will choose to trust and obey God, it will bring God's blessings upon the whole family. You can see this truth very clearly in Proverbs 31:10-31 and Psalm 128:1-4. God wouldn't have given these promises to the husband or wife who chooses to obey Him if His influence upon their family wasn't powerful enough to bring His Word to pass. God will always move on a spouse's heart and create in them a desire to obey Him for the benefit of the spouse who has chosen to trust Him.

Examine this truth in the following scriptures:

Read Proverbs 21:1. *The king's heart is in the hand of the Lord as are the watercourses; He turns it whichever way He will.* (AMP)

Will God turn a person's heart? How does this scripture build your confidence in the power of God's influence?_____

_____

According to the original Hebrew language, the word translated "heart" in this scripture literally means the feelings, the will, and even the intellect of a person. *Lexical Aids to the Old Testament* says this word means "the seat of the will." Therefore, you can see from this verse that God will turn a person's heart. There are instances in which He will turn a person's mind, will and emotions in the direction that He wills. You learned previously in II Corinthians 1:12 that God's grace is His influence upon a person's soul (their mind, will and emotions) which turns them toward Jesus and increases them in Christian character. What you must understand, then, is that it's through the prayer of faith that God's grace becomes available to work on a person's heart. James 5:16 says, *pray [also] for one another...The earnest (heartfelt, continued) prayer of a righteous man makes tremendous power available.* (AMP) This is why God instructs us in I Timothy 2:1-4 to pray for those in authority over us. God's power works in a person's life through the prayers of His people.

Proverbs 21:1 clearly reveals that God has the power to turn your spouse's heart. You can't change your spouse, but as you begin to pray in faith for them, God will influence their heart and bring about a change in their life.

If you've been unhappy with your marriage relationship and you want to receive God's promises for your marriage, you mustn't focus on your spouse's present attitude. If you continue to focus on what they're saying or doing, you'll become discouraged and feel hopeless. But if you'll put your trust in the power of God and what He has promised you, God will influence your spouse's heart and turn it in the direction that He wills. *Influence* means the power to act upon a person and bring about a result without using force. God's influence is so powerful that it will bring about a change in your spouse without forcing or making them. If you'll pray God's Word over your spouse, and put your confidence in the power of His influence, your prayers will be powerful and effective! He will perform His will in their life.

You can see the power of God's influence again in Philippians 2:13: *It is God which worketh in you both to will and to do of His good pleasure.* (KJV)

The original Greek word translated "will" in this scripture means "to choose" or "to be willing." The *Lexical Aids* says this word means "not only willing something, but pressing on to action." With this in mind, you can better understand what God's power can accomplish in a person's life. This verse clearly reveals that when God's power works within a person, He not only influences them to choose His ways, but He also presses them on to do what they have chosen.

Phillipians 2:13 in the *Amplified Bible* gives an even clearer understanding of the power of God's influence: *"It is God Who is all the while effectually at work in you — energizing and creating in you the power and desire — both to will and to work for His good pleasure and satisfaction and delight.* (AMP)

This verse shows the power God's influence can have on a person's life. God can effectually work within His people and create in them the desire to choose His ways, and He also gives them the power to do so. However, many people don't have God's power at work in their life or in the life of their spouse because they haven't asked. James 4:2 says, *You do not have because you do not ask.* When you pray and ask God to create in you and your spouse the desire and power to do what pleases Him, His grace will be at work influencing both of you to become what He wants you to be. You can be confident in God to perform His will in your marriage because you and your spouse are joint-heirs to the life-changing power of His grace (I Peter 3:7).

For further study on the power of God's influence see John 6:44 (AMP), Ezekiel 36:26-27, Jeremiah 32:40, Phillipians 1:6, Hebrews 13:20-21, & Romans 9:16-19.

One of the most profound truths found in God's Word concerning your marriage relationship is that Jesus redeemed you from a curse upon your marriage.

In Deuteronomy 28:15-67 the Bible reveals the curses that God said would come upon His people if they chose to disobey His laws. It's called the curse of the law. Verses 30, 54 and 56 tell about the curse that would come upon the marriage relationship. These verses say that the enemy would oppress them; the husband would be evil and begrudging toward his wife, and she would be evil and begrudging toward her husband. If you're living in an unhappy marriage and you and your spouse aren't being loving and kind toward one another, and if strife is between you, you're living under a curse.

Galatians 3:13-14 reveals the good news of the gospel of Jesus: *Christ redeemed us from the curse of the law by becoming a curse for us, for it is written: "Cursed is everyone who is hung on a tree." He redeemed us in order that the blessing given to Abraham might come to the Gentiles through Christ Jesus, so that by faith we might receive the promise of the Spirit.* (NIV)

The blood of Jesus redeemed you from the curse of the law, which includes the curse upon your marriage. He took the curse upon Himself so the blessing of God can come upon your relationship. The redemptive work of Jesus covers every area of your life — a blessed marriage, blessed children, healing, financial abundance, emotional healing, deliverance from bondage, and spiritual blessings. Jesus purchased them all for you. This is why He is the answer to whatever problem you face.

Jesus paid the price for you to receive God's blessing upon your marriage relationship. If you'll put your trust in Him concerning this area of your life, you'll receive what He purchased for you. No one can stand in the way of you receiving what has been promised to you because of Him. If you'll believe this truth with your heart and speak it to be true in your life, you'll receive God's perfect will for your marriage.

According to I John 5:14-15, God has promised that if you'll pray for your marriage according to His will, you can be confident that He will grant what you've requested. God will begin to change you and your spouse as you depend on His grace. When you choose to cast all your cares on God and completely trust in His promises, you'll receive His perfect plan for your marriage. God is able to do exceeding abundantly above all that you desire, hope, or dream, according to His power which is at work in your life (Ephesians 3:20). You may think this seems impossible, that your marriage could never be this good, but you must remember that nothing's impossible to those who believe, and absolutely nothing is impossible for God (Mark 9:23)!

II. God has given you promises for your children.

Read Proverbs 22:6.

What does God promise you in this scripture?_____

_____

Read Deuteronomy 6:4-7.

How does God instruct you to train your children to follow after Him?

_____

_____

_____

Read Proverbs 29: 15 & 17.

What will bring wisdom to your child? What does God promise if you'll correct your children?_____

_____

_____

Read Proverbs 22:15.

What does God promise will drive foolishness from your child?_____

_____

God promises that the rod of correction will bring wisdom to your children, and that they will give you rest. However, God warns in Proverbs 22:8 that the rod of anger will fail. If you discipline your children in anger, you won't reap the benefits that God's Word promises. You must correct them with love. Read Ephesians 6:4 and Colossians 3:21.

Isaiah 54:13 says *all your [spiritual] children shall be disciples [taught by the Lord and obedient to His will], and great shall be the peace and undisturbed composure of your children.* (AMP)

What promise has God given you in this scripture concerning your children? _____

_____

_____

This is a powerful promise from God concerning your children. Remember, in order to receive His promises, you must believe them. Those who believe this promise with their hearts and confess it to be true are the ones who will experience it in their children's lives.

Read Isaiah 44:3-5.

What does God promise He will do concerning your children?_____

_____

_____

This scripture says that God will pour His Spirit upon your children and they will say, "I belong to the Lord." In Ezekiel 36:27 God says, *"I will put My Spirit within you and cause you to walk in My statues, and you shall heed My ordinances, and do them."* (AMP) If you'll put your trust in God's promise, you can be confident that He will pour His Spirit upon your children and create in them the desire and power to follow His ways.

For your children to be taken captive by the enemy is a curse of the law (Deuteronomy 28:32, 41). Galatians 3:13-14 says that Jesus redeemed you from this curse. Because of Jesus, you've inherited God's promise that His righteousness shall be with your children and your grandchildren (Psalm 103:17).

Read Isaiah 59:21.

What covenant has God made with you concerning your children and your grandchildren?

_____

_____

Read Psalm 112:1-2.

When you walk in the fear of the Lord, and delight in obeying His Word, what does God promise you?_____

_____

Read Jeremiah 31:15-17.

If your children are grown and aren't serving God, what hope can you find from the promise found in verses 16 and 17?_____

_____

_____

Read Isaiah 49:25: *But this is what the Lord says:..I will contend with those who contend with you, and your children I will save.* (NIV)

In this scripture God promises to save your children. God can be trusted to do what He has spoken, for in Isaiah 46:11 He says, "Yes, *I have spoken, and I will bring it to pass; I have purposed it and I will do it.*" (AMP)

God has promised that if you'll trust and obey Him, your children will be mighty and blessed upon the earth. He will pour His Spirit upon them, and they won't depart from His ways. They'll be taught by God, obedient to His will, and their peace shall be great. God has made a covenant with you. He has promised that His Spirit, which is upon you, and His Word, which He has put in your mouth, will also be spoken by your children and your grandchildren. You can rest in God's promises concerning your children and receive the wonderful plan He has for their lives by simply trusting in the faithfulness of your Heavenly Father.

SUMMARY

God has given you many wonderful promises. Many of God's people fail to receive His best because they lack knowledge and don't believe. You can inherit God's promises for your marriage and your children if you'll put your complete trust in His Word. All of God's promises belong to you through Christ Jesus; however, you must say the "Amen, so be it in my life!" When you put your confidence in God's Word, He will watch over it to perform it in your life.

PERSONAL APPLICATION

How can you receive God's promises? (Hebrews 6:12)_____

_____

What are the two parts of faith? (II Corinthians 4:13)_____

_____

Believing God's promises in your heart +
confessing them to be true with your mouth = **FAITH**

Patience is the quality that refuses to give up. It's characterized by a determination to receive God's best for your marriage and your children. In order to receive God's promises you must be determined to receive all that He has planned for you.

What promise did God give you in Mark 11:22-23 concerning speaking His Word over your marriage and your children?_____

_____

_____

Begin to confidently confess God's promises to be true in your life:

- My children shall be disciples of the Lord, taught by the Him and obedient to His will; and their peace and undisturbed composure shall be great.

- God's Spirit and His Word shall not depart from my mouth, nor from my children or my grandchildren from this time on and forever.

- I will correct my children, and they'll give me peace. They will be a delight to my heart.

- I'll train my children to follow God and when they're grown, they won't depart from His ways. God will pour His Spirit upon my children and they'll say, "I belong to the Lord."

Begin to pray God's will for your marriage and expect God's grace to do a powerful work in your life.

A WIFE'S PRAYER

Lord, I realize that it's only by Your grace working in me that I'm able to become the virtuous woman You want me to be. I ask You to create in me the desire and ability to love my husband with Your love. Help me see the best in him. I pray that You'll help me live a godly life in front of him — loving, respecting, praising, and encouraging him. I submit my life to Your Word because I want to please You in this area of my life. I thank You that You've made us joint-heirs to Your grace. I trust that Your grace is at work in my husband, creating in him the desire and ability to love me like Christ loves the Church. As You do a work in him, he'll be patient and kind, never boastful or proud. He'll be affectionate toward me. He'll see the best in me and think I'm the greatest of them all.

I have confidence in You, Lord, because You've promised that if I pray according to Your will, You'll answer my prayer. I'm convinced of this very thing: that You Who began a good work in us will continue until the day of Jesus Christ, developing that good work and bringing it to full completion in us (Philippians 1:6). Thank You, Lord, for performing Your perfect will in my marriage. In Jesus' name, Amen.

Continue to thank God for the work He's doing before you see it in the natural. Speak the "Amen" to God's promises.

A HUSBAND'S PRAYER

Lord, I ask you to help me love my wife like Christ loves the Church. I won't be harsh or resentful toward her because I have Your love shed abroad in my heart and I'm able to love her with your unconditional love. I see the best in her and I appreciate the gift she is to me. Help me meet her needs emotionally, financially, and spiritually, for You've called me to be the head of my home. Lord, I know that as I walk in obedience to You in my marriage, my wife will become a fruitful vine within my home because You've promised it. She'll respect, appreciate and love me with your unconditional love. She'll be my helpmate and a crowning joy in my life. I ask that Your grace be at work in her creating the desire and ability to become the virtuous woman that I want her to be. Lord, I thank You for performing Your perfect will in my marriage, for it's only by Your grace at work in us that we're able to become all that you want us to be. Thank you, Lord, for Your grace. In Jesus' name, Amen.

Continue to thank God for the work He's performing in your marriage before you see it in the natural. Remember, when you add real faith to God's promises, you'll believe it in your heart and boldly declare it to be true with your mouth. Begin to say the "Amen" to God's promises.

If you want to see your spouse grow spiritually, you can begin to pray Colossians 1:9-12 over them. God's grace will begin to create in them the desire and ability to draw closer to Him. When you pray God's Word, you're praying His will. Therefore, you have His promise that He will hear and answer your prayer according to I John 5:14-15.

Lesson 5

God's Promises for Your Unsaved Family, and His Protection

PURPOSE

To realize what God has promised concerning the salvation of your family and to study God's promises of protection so you won't lack knowledge of His will for your life.

OVERVIEW

God's will has been revealed through His Word. As you study, you'll learn what God wants for you in every area of your life. As you learn about His promises for your unsaved family members, and His promises of protection, you'll continue to realize the wonderful plan He has for you. The Bible teaches that you'll receive God's will for your life if you'll add faith and patience to all He has promised.

DISCUSSION

I. God promises the salvation of your family.

Read Job 22:30. *He will even deliver the one [for whom you intercede] who is not innocent; yes, he will be delivered through the cleanness of your hands.* (AMP)

What promise do you find in this scripture?_____

_____

_____

This scripture states that through your prayers, God will deliver those for whom you intercede.

Read Colossians 1:13: *[The Father] has delivered and drawn us to Himself out of the control and the dominion of darkness and has transferred us into the kingdom of the Son of His love.* (AMP)

From what will God deliver your unsaved family? What change will take place in their lives when you begin to pray?_____

_____

_____

Read I Timothy 2:1-4.

In verse 1, what does God urge and admonish you to do? _____

_____

_____

What is God's desire and will concerning your unsaved family? (verse 4) _____

_____

_____

I Timothy 2:4 clearly indicates that it's God's will for your unsaved family to receive salvation. Considering this, what confidence can you have before God when you pray that they will be delivered from the powers of darkness? Read I John 5:14-15.

_____

_____

In I Timothy 2:1, God urges you to pray and intercede on behalf of those who are unsaved. He has promised to deliver the one for whom you intercede. God moves through the prayers of His people. If you'll be diligent in praying for your unsaved family members, God will draw them to salvation. When you pray according to His will, you can have confidence that God will answer your prayers.

Will God put the desire in a person's heart to be saved?

Read John 6:44. *No one is able to come to Me unless the Father Who sent Me attracts and draws him and gives him the desire to come to Me, and [then] I will raise him up [from the dead] at the last day.* (AMP)

What does God have to do in your unsaved loved one's life before they're able to come to Jesus?_____

_____

This scripture clearly shows that a person can't come to Jesus unless God is at work in their heart. When a person comes to Jesus, it's because the Father draws him and *gives him the desire* to receive salvation. God will give this desire to your unsaved family when you begin to pray for them. God doesn't want anyone to perish. He wants everyone to come to repentance (II Peter 3:9).

Matthew 21:22 says *whatever you ask for in prayer, having faith and [really] believing, you will receive.* (AMP)

This scripture teaches that when you ask God to draw your family to salvation, you must have faith and really believe that He will do it. It's only when you ask in faith that you'll receive the answer to your prayer.

James 1:6-7 says: *6But when he asks, he must believe and not doubt, because he who doubts is like a wave of the sea, blown and tossed by the wind. 7That man should not think he will receive anything from the Lord.* (NIV)

When you pray for the salvation of your unsaved family, you must be confident that God is at work in their lives. If you doubt that He is faithful to answer your request, your prayer will be ineffective. You must know that God will deliver them from the power of darkness and transfer them into the kingdom of His Son. He will do this when you put your absolute trust in His ability to draw them to salvation. Remember, nothing is impossible with God (Luke 1:37).

Hebrews 6:12 states that you must add faith and patience to God's promises before you'll receive them in your life. Patience is the quality that refuses to give up. It refuses to surrender to circumstances. You must not allow the attitudes and actions of your unsaved family to cause you to doubt that God is actively at work in their hearts.

Read Acts 16:31.

What promise is found in this scripture concerning your family?_____
_____
_____

The original Greek word translated "house" in this scripture means "family" or those who are related to you.

This scripture reveals that if you'll put your trust in Jesus, God not only promises your salvation, but He also promises to draw your family and relatives to salvation as well.

Make a list of your family members who are unsaved.

_____
_____
_____
_____

Remember, according to II Corinthians 1:20, all of God's promises belong to you. However, you must say the "Amen, so be it" to claim your family's salvation according to the promises of God's Word. When you add faith and patience to God's promises, they'll become a reality in your life. Nothing is impossible to those who believe! (Mark 9:23)

What's happening in the lives of those who haven't received salvation?

Read II Corinthians 4:4. *For the god of this world has blinded the unbelievers' minds [that they should not discern the truth], preventing them from seeing the illuminating light of the Gospel of the glory of Christ (the Messiah), Who is the Image and Likeness of God.* (AMP)

According to this scripture, why aren't your loved ones saved? Who's influencing their lives?

_____
_____

The Bible says that those who are unsaved are under the control of the prince of the power of the air. A demon spirit is at work in the lives of those who haven't received salvation.

This truth is revealed in Ephesians 2:2: *In which at one time you walked [habitually]. You were following the course and fashion of this world [were under the sway of the tendency of this present age], following the prince of the power of the air. [You were obedient to and under the control of] the [demon] spirit that still constantly works in the sons of disobedience [the careless, the rebellious, and the unbelieving, who go against the purposes of God].* (AMP)

Explain what this scripture is saying about the influence the devil has over your unsaved loved ones. _____

_____

_____

These verses have clearly shown that the reason people are unsaved is not just because of a decision that they've made based on their own will to choose. Instead, it's actually the enemy blinding them and preventing them from seeing the truth. They're actually under the control of the enemy.

Many times God's people use the excuse that their unsaved family members have a will, and God won't change their will. It's true that God won't make a person receive Jesus; however, when a person's eyes are opened to the truth of what Jesus has done for them, God puts the desire in them to want to serve Him. (John 6:44 AMP)

Your unsaved loved ones are under the control of the enemy; however, the good news is that God's people have authority over all the power the enemy possesses.

Read Luke 10:17-19.

What truth, concerning your authority over the enemy, is revealed in these verses?

_____

_____

Matthew 18:18 says *whatever you forbid and declare to be improper and unlawful on earth must be what is already forbidden in heaven, and whatever you permit and declare proper and lawful on earth must be what is already permitted in heaven.* (AMP)

God has given you authority over the enemy. You can forbid him from continuing to blind and control the minds of your unsaved loved ones. Since James 5:16 says that the earnest, heartfelt, continued prayer of a righteous man makes tremendous power available, you can know without doubt that God's power becomes available to you as you begin to pray.

What begins to happen in the lives of your unsaved loved ones when you begin to pray in faith concerning their salvation?

Job 22:30 _____

_____

Colossians 1:13 _____

_____

John 6:44 _____

_____

We've established the fact that a person's will is either being influenced by the enemy or by God. If no one is trusting God concerning a person's salvation, then that person's will is being influenced by the devil and the following is taking place in their life:

- The god of this world is influencing them. The enemy is blinding the unbeliever's mind so that they can't discern the truth. The devil is preventing them from seeing the gospel of Jesus. (II Corinthians 4:4)

- A demon spirit is constantly at work in the unbeliever's life. That person is under the control of the devil. (Ephesians 2:2)

On the other hand, if someone is diligently praying with confidence for an unbeliever, and is trusting in God's promises, then that person's will is being influenced by God and the following is taking place in their life:

- The enemy is forbidden from continuing to blind and control that person. He can no longer blind them from the truth (Matthew 18:18).

- God begins to draw and attract the person to Jesus. He puts the desire in them to come to Jesus and receive salvation (John 6:44).

- God will deliver them and draw them to Himself, out of the control and dominion of darkness, and will transfer them into the kingdom of His Son (Colossians 1:13; Job 22:30).

Have you had confidence in God's ability and power to draw your unsaved loved ones to salvation? Or have you allowed the attitudes and actions of your unsaved family to cause you to doubt that they'll come to Jesus?

Now that you realize the devil is influencing their lives, will you allow him to continue to blind and control them? Or will you forbid him from continuing to deceive them, and trust God to bring to pass His will for their lives?

The reason they're unsaved is because the enemy has blinded their eyes from the truth. However, the reason they'll receive salvation is because you'll begin to intercede for them and you'll confidently expect God to keep His promise.

Begin to pray God's Word over your unsaved loved ones. Confidently expect them to receive Jesus because of what God has promised you. When you pray God's Word, you're praying His will. Remember, God's Word won't return void because He watches over His Word to perform it (Isaiah 55:11; Jeremiah 1:12). James 5:16 says that the earnest, heartfelt, continued prayer of a righteous man makes tremendous power available which is dynamic in its working!

II. God promises protection.

Read Psalm 91.

Psalm 91:1-2 explains that when you put your trust in God's promise to protect you, you'll abide under the shadow of the Almighty.

If you'll make God your refuge and your fortress by putting your trust in His protection, what does God promise you?

verse 3 _____

_____

verse 4 _____

_____

verse 5 _____

_____

verses 6-8 _____

_____

_____

verses 9-12 (Read Luke 4:10-11.) _____

_____

_____

verse 13 (Read Luke 10:19.) _____

_____

verses 14-16 _____

_____

_____

Proverbs 12:21 says *no [actual] evil, misfortune, or calamity will come upon the righteous.* (AMP)

Proverbs 19:23 also tells us *the reverent, worshipful fear of the Lord leads to life, and he who has it shall rest satisfied; he cannot be visited with [actual] evil.* (AMP)

What promise is found in both of these scriptures? _____

_____

According to Psalm 91:10, when you put your trust in God's protection, no evil, disease, or harm can come near you or your family because God will command His angels to take charge over you and protect you.

Psalm 145:20 says *the Lord preserveth all them that love him.* (KJV)

According to the original Hebrew text, the word translated "preserveth" in this verse means "protect." God puts a hedge of protection around you when you put your trust in His Word.

Read Proverbs 29:25. *The fear of man brings a snare, but whoever leans on, trusts in, and puts his confidence in the Lord is safe and set on high.* (AMP)

What will fear bring into your life? _____

What will happen if you will put your trust in God's protection?_____

_____

You mustn't allow fear to rule your life. As you can see from this verse, fear has the opposite effect of trust. Fear opens the door for harm.

What must you do in order to receive God's promise of protection? (Psalm 91:9-11)

_____

_____

Is fear present in your life when you're truly trusting God? (Psalm 91:5)_____

_____

The only fear anyone should have is the fear of not putting their complete trust in God and resting in His promises. Hebrews 4:1 says, *Therefore, while the promise of entering His rest still holds and is offered [today], let us be afraid [to distrust it].* (AMP)

What should you be afraid to do?_____

_____

Psalm 4:8 says: *In peace I will both lie down and sleep, for You, Lord, alone make me dwell in safety and confident trust.* (AMP)

Proverbs 1:33 says: *But whoever listens to me will live in safety and be at ease, without fear of harm.* (NIV)

What truth is found in these scriptures?_____

_____

When you rest in God's promise of protection, you'll live in safety. You'll have no fear of harm. You'll be confident that He has commanded His angels to protect you in all your ways.

SUMMARY

You can trust God to draw your unsaved family to salvation. He will deliver them from the control of the devil and transfer them into the kingdom of His Son when you begin to pray. You can inherit God's promises for your unsaved loved ones and His promise of protection if you'll put your complete trust in the integrity of His Word. All of God's promises belong to you; however, you must say the "Amen, so be it in my life!"

PERSONAL APPLICATION

What has God promised concerning your unsaved family's salvation?_____

_____

_____

_____

Begin to pray for your family's salvation according to the will of God, and confidently expect them to receive Jesus.

PRAYER

Lord, I bring _____ before You today and I ask You to fulfill your promise in their lives. You said you would deliver those I pray for. I ask you to deliver them from the control and dominion of darkness, draw them to Yourself and translate them into the kingdom of Your Son. It's Your will that _____ be saved and come to the knowledge of the truth. I forbid the enemy from continuing to blind them, for You've given me authority over all the power the enemy possesses. He can no longer prevent them from seeing the Gospel of Jesus Christ. You'll open their eyes so they can see the truth. I pray that You'll give them the desire to serve You. You said that if I trust in Jesus, I would be saved, and all of my family. Thank you Lord for Your promise. I thank you Father for the confidence I have in You to perform Your will in their lives. I see them serving You. I trust in Your Word and I believe that it won't return void, but that it will accomplish what You've sent it forth to do. In Jesus' name, Amen.

Begin to thank God for your family's salvation as though it were already done. Continue to thank God that the eyes of their understanding are being opened. Ephesians 1:16-19 and Ephesians 3:16-20 are wonderful scriptures to use for prayer for them. As you pray God's Word, His grace will be at work in their hearts drawing them to salvation.

II Corinthians 1:12 says *by the grace of God (the unmerited favor and merciful kindness by which God, exerting His holy influence upon souls, turns them to Christ, and keeps, strengthens, and increases them in Christian virtues).* (AMP)

You can see from this scripture that when you begin to pray in faith for your family's salvation, God's grace will influence their wills and turn them to Christ. You can be confident that they'll receive Jesus when you put your absolute trust in Him.

What has God promised you concerning His protection?

_____

_____

_____

_____

Renew your mind to God's promises concerning His protection. Meditate on Psalm 91. Begin to say "Amen" to God's promises of protection:

The Lord is my refuge and my fortress; in Him will I trust. He will deliver me from the snare of the enemy and from deadly diseases. He will cover me with His feathers and His faithfulness will be my shield. I will not be afraid, for though a thousand may fall at my right side and ten thousand at my left, it will not come near me. I have made the Lord my refuge and I have put my complete trust in Him; therefore, no evil will befall me, no plague or tragedy will come near my home. For He has commanded his angels to take special charge over me and protect me in all my ways. (Adapted from Psalm 91:1-11.)

Lesson 6
God's Promises for Your Health and Finances

PURPOSE

To discover what God has promised concerning your health and finances so you can fully understand what Jesus has provided for you.

OVERVIEW

As you continue to search God's Word, you'll realize that your Heavenly Father has made provision for you to walk in health. He has also provided many promises to abundantly supply all of your needs. If you'll choose to completely trust in His promises and be determined to receive them, you'll partake of the inheritance that is yours as a child of God.

DISCUSSION

I.   God promises health and healing.

Read Proverbs 4:20-22.

What four things does God instruct you to do?

_____

_____

_____

What does He promise this will produce in your life? (verse 22) _____

_____

In these scriptures, God reveals how you can receive healing for your body. We'll take a closer look at the four things that God instructs you to do:

1. Pay attention to His Word.

2. Listen closely to what He has promised you. Meditate and think upon His Word.

3. Keep your eyes focused on His promises. Don't allow your problem to distract you from His promise. Don't let His Word out of your sight.

4. Put His Word in your heart by meditating upon it day and night. (Read Psalm 119:97.)

God's Word is medicine to your body. It will bring health and healing to all your flesh as you meditate upon it and declare it to be true in your life. This is what God has promised, and He doesn't lie. If you'll put God's Word in your heart and apply it to your life, you'll walk in divine health.

Read Proverbs 3:7-8: *Do not be wise in your own eyes; fear the Lord and shun evil. This will bring health to your body and nourishment to your bones.* (NIV)

According to this scripture, what will bring health to your body? _____

_____

_____

Obedience to God's Word will bring health to your body. When you fear the Lord, it means that you turn away from any attitude or action that is displeasing to Him. When you follow after the wisdom in God's Word, He promises you good health.

Proverbs 14:30 says *a calm and undisturbed mind and heart are the life and health of the body, but envy, jealousy, and wrath are like rottenness of the bones.* (AMP)

According to this scripture, what brings life and health to your body? _____

_____

What can bring sickness to your body? _____

_____

Read Psalm 103:1-3.

What are the benefits of being a child of God? (verse 3) _____

_____

Many Christians have no problem believing that God will forgive all of their sins, yet it's difficult for them to believe that He'll heal all of their diseases. This Scripture clearly indicates that it's God's desire not only to forgive your sins but also to heal your body. God doesn't want you to forget the benefits of being His child. Just as you trust Him to forgive your sins, you must also trust Him to heal your body.

Deuteronomy 28:15, and 58-61 reveal that sickness and disease are a curse of the law; however, Galatians 3:13-14 teaches that Jesus redeemed you from that curse. He took the curse upon Himself so you can receive the blessing of divine health!

Read Isaiah 53:5.

According to this verse, what did Jesus do for you? Personalize this scripture.

_____

_____

_____

Again you can see that Jesus not only paid the price for your sins to be forgiven, but He also paid the price for your body to be healed. This scripture says *with his stripes we are healed.* Some Christians have taught that this verse refers to spiritual healing. But in the gospel according to Matthew, the Bible clearly indicates that the stripes that wounded Jesus brought healing to our physical bodies.

Read Matthew 8:16-17.

These verses refer to what is written in Isaiah 53:5. According to verse 16, what did Jesus do when the sick were brought to Him?_____

_____

According to verse 17, what scripture did Jesus fulfill when He healed the sick?

_____

What two things does this scripture reveal that Jesus has done for you?

_____

_____

Read Matthew 9:35.

Jesus went about preaching the gospel. According to this scripture, what did the gospel include?_____

_____

The gospel not only includes forgiveness of sin, it also includes healing of sickness. Jesus clearly reveals this in Matthew 9:35. When Jesus preached the gospel, He healed the sick. Some of God's people believe that Jesus no longer heals today. However, what truth is revealed in Hebrews 13:8?_____

_____

Read James 5:14-16.

What does verse 14 say you should do if you're sick?_____

_____

What kind of prayer will make you well? (verse 15)_____

_____

According to verse 16, what two things must you do to receive healing? _____

_____

_____

Once again we can see a connection between forgiveness of sin and the healing of our bodies. Jesus provided the blessing of both.

How does the Word of God describe the prayer of a righteous man?_____

_____

Many times symptoms don't change immediately. Often people are looking for an instantaneous recovery, and if that doesn't happen, they think God didn't answer their prayer. However, you must believe that God has heard and answered your prayer before you see any change take place in your body. Mark 11:24 says *whatever you ask for in prayer, believe that you have received it, and it will be yours.* (NIV)

You must add patience to your faith. You must have the quality that refuses to give up. Patience is what will keep your faith active until healing is manifested in your body. Healing is part of your inheritance as a child of God. Don't allow the lack of patience to cause you to fail to receive what Jesus purchased and provided for you.

II. God has given promises for your finances.

Read Matthew 6:25-33.

In verse 25 what does God tell you not to worry about?_____
_____
_____

What does God want you to believe about Him? (verses 26 & 30) _____
_____
_____

Verses 31 and 32 explain that the world diligently seeks after material things. What type of material things does the world seek?_____
_____
_____

In verse 33, what promise did God give you concerning the material things that the world seeks? What's the condition to His promise? _____
_____

In this passage of scripture, God says that when you choose to worry about your needs, you aren't fully trusting Him. When you were a child, you didn't worry about your needs being met because you trusted your parents to take care of you. God wants you to have this same confidence in Him. Phillipians 4:19 says: *But my God shall supply all your needs according to his riches in glory by Christ Jesus.* (KJV) God is your Heavenly Father and you're His child. He'll take care of you when you put your trust in Him.

Matthew 6:32 explains that people in the world diligently seek material things (good food, nice clothes, beautiful houses, etc.). God doesn't want you to seek these things; however, He did promise you that if you diligently seek to please Him and to promote His kingdom, then He will bless you with everything the world seeks. This is a powerful promise from God!

Solomon gives an example of what you should seek and desire most in your life.

Read II Chronicles 1:8-12.

What was Solomon's greatest desire? What did He want from God? (verse 10)_____
_____
_____

God was pleased with Solomon's request and because of this, promised him what?

_____

_____

God doesn't want you to seek riches, wealth, or honor. His desire is that you seek Him and His wisdom. Riches and wealth alone can never satisfy or bring true happiness and joy. However, if you'll desire and seek God's wisdom, He has given you a promise similar to what He gave Solomon.

You can see this truth in Proverbs 8:10-12, & 17-18: *10Choose my instruction instead of silver, knowledge rather than choice gold, 11for wisdom is more precious than rubies, and nothing you desire can compare with her. 12"I, wisdom, dwell together with prudence.....17I love those who love me, and those who seek me find me. 18With me are riches and honor, enduring wealth and prosperity."* (NIV)

In verse 18, what does God's Word say will be evident in the life of the person who seeks His wisdom?_____

_____

Where can you find the wisdom of God?

Many people in the world aren't followers of God but they have great wealth; however, without the wisdom of God operating in their lives, they aren't able to fully enjoy it. The Bible warns you not to envy sinners. You must realize that true joy, peace, happiness, and fulfillment can only be found in God. Riches alone can't satisfy.

When God blesses His people financially, He gives them the power to enjoy it. It's just one of the many blessings that God gives to those who will trust and obey His Word.

Ecclesiastes 5:18-19 reveals this truth: *18Then I realized that it is good and proper for a man to eat and drink, and to find satisfaction in his toilsome labor under the sun during the few days of life God has given him — for this is his lot. 19Moreover, when God gives any man wealth and possessions, and enables him to enjoy them, to accept his lot and be happy in his work — this is a gift of God.* NIV

How does verse 19 describe a gift of God? _____

_____

_____

Who does God reward? Who will receive this gift from God? Read Hebrews 11:6.

_____

_____

Many scriptures throughout the Bible prove God's will for His people in the area of finances. God wants His people to prosper. He has proven this by what He has promised in His Word.

- Psalm 34:9-10 says: *Fear the Lord, you his saints, for those who fear him lack nothing. The lions may grow weak and hungry, but those who seek the Lord lack no good thing.* (NIV)

- Psalm 37:25-26 says: *I was young and now I am old, yet I have never seen the righteous forsaken or their children begging bread. They are always generous and lend freely; their children will be blessed.* (NIV)

- Proverbs 22:4 says: *Humility and the fear of the Lord bring wealth and honor and life.* (NIV)

- Isaiah 1:19 says: *If you will only let me help you, if you will only obey, then I will make you rich!* (TLB)

- Proverbs 3:9-10 says: *Honor the Lord with your capital and sufficiency [from righteous labors] and with the first fruits of all your income; 10So shall your storage places be filled with plenty.* (AMP)

- Psalm 112:1 & 3 says: *Praise the Lord. Blessed is the man who fears the Lord, who finds great delight in His commands. Wealth and riches are in his house, and his righteousness endures forever.* (NIV)

Look back over the scriptures you just read and examine the condition and the promise found in each scripture.

	The Condition	The Promise
Psalm 34:9-10:		
Psalm 37:25-26		
Proverbs 22:4		
Isaiah 1:19		
Proverbs 3:9 -10		
Psalm 112:1 & 3		

Throughout the Bible, these promises of financial abundance were evident in the lives of God's people who chose to trust and obey Him. God performed His Word in each of their lives. By examining the following people, you'll gain a greater understanding of God's will for you:

- Abraham: Genesis 24:34-35
- Isaac: Genesis 26:12-14
- Joseph: Genesis 39:2-3
- God's people who entered the promised land: Joshua 22:1-8
- King David: I Chronicles 29:26-28
- King Jehoshaphat: II Chronicles 17:3-5
- King Hezekiah: II Chronicles 32:27-29

What was evident in the life of each one of these persons? How did God bless their obedience?

Now that you realize God has always blessed His covenant people with financial abundance, do you believe that He wants to bless you, a covenant child of God, in this same way? Why or why not? _____

_____

The Bible warns Christians not to fall into deception by following the traditions of men and disregarding the teachings of Christ (Colossians 2:8). Unfortunately, many still believe that religion and poverty go hand-in-hand. Romans 12:2 tells us not to be conformed to this world or its superficial customs (even church traditions or customs) but instead to be *transformed (changed) by the [entire] renewal of your mind—by its new ideals and its new attitude—so that you may* **prove** *[for yourselves] what is the good and acceptable and perfect will of God, even the thing which is good and acceptable and perfect [in His sight for you].* (AMP) The Jews to whom Paul preached were commended in Acts 17:11 for searching and examining the Scriptures daily to make sure that what they were being taught was true. In the same manner, it's your responsibility to search the Bible to confirm that what you are taught is true.

Deuteronomy 28:43-48 reveals that financial lack is a curse of the law; however, in Galatians 3:13-14 the Bible teaches that Jesus redeemed you from the curse of lack. He did this so that you could receive the blessings of abundance that were promised to Abraham and his descendants.

Read Deuteronomy 28:1-13.

With what blessings has God promised to fill your life if you'll choose to trust and obey His Word? Remember, you're a seed of Abraham and an heir to all that God has promised.

_____

_____

_____

_____

_____

_____

_____

God's Word clearly reveals that He wants you to be financially prosperous. To deny or reject this fact is to deny that His Word is true. Whether or not you partake of the promises of financial abundance depends entirely on you. You can choose to reject His promises because of the teachings of men, or you can choose to add faith and patience to His Word and claim His promises to be true in your life. Your decision will determine whether or not you partake of His plan for this area of your life.

If you want to receive the financial abundance that God has promised, what should you ask God for? Read James 1:5. _____

Proverbs 8:12 says: *I wisdom dwell with prudence, and find out knowledge of witty inventions.* (KJV)

When you receive God's wisdom, what will you discover?_____

_____

God has always blessed His people through the works of their hands. He gave them wisdom regarding what to do; and as they obeyed God, they received abundant blessings in their lives. As you ask for wisdom and truly believe that God will give it to you, He will give you ideas and plans that will prosper and succeed. God will show you what to do, and the steps to take to bring increase in your life. You'll have knowledge of clever inventions or ideas that will bring abundant blessing into your life. Read Deuteronomy 30:8-9.

Why does God want you to experience abundance in your finances? The answer can be found in His Word.

Read II Corinthians 9:6-11.

What promise is revealed in verse 6? _____

_____

What kind of giver does God love? (verse 7) _____

_____

What will God's grace produce in your life? (verse 8) _____

_____

_____

II Corinthians 9:11 says *you will be made rich in every way so that you can be generous on every occasion, and through us your generosity will result in thanksgiving to God.* (NIV)

According to this verse, why does God want to bless you financially? _____

_____

_____

In these scriptures, God has promised to abundantly supply all of your needs so you can give generously to others. This is the reason so many promises are given to the generous giver. God's purpose for prospering His people is so they can promote the gospel of Jesus Christ and give to those in need.

Luke 6:38 says *give, and it will be given to you. A good measure, pressed down, shaken together and running over, will be poured into your lap. For with the measure you use, it will be measured to you.* (NIV)

Proverbs 11:24-25 says *one man gives freely, yet gains even more; another withholds unduly, but comes to poverty. A generous man will prosper; he who refreshes others will himself be refreshed.* (NIV)

What promise is given to the generous man in both of these scriptures? _____

_____

_____

Read I Timothy 6:17-19.

These verses tell you that "God gives us richly all things." Why does God bless you abundantly? Two reasons can be found in this passage.

verse 17: _____

verse 18: _____

Read Deuteronomy 8:6-18.

What is God's plan for His people?

verses 7-9: _____

_____

_____

verse 12: _____

verse 13: _____

What warning does God give in verses 10-14, & 17? _____

_____

_____

_____

When God blesses you financially, what does He want you to remember? (verse 18)

_____

_____

Why does God give His people the ability to obtain wealth? (verse 18)

_____

In Genesis 12:2 God made a covenant with Abraham: *I will bless you [with abundant increase of favors] and make your name famous and distinguished, and you will be a blessing [dispensing good to others].* (AMP)

In Genesis 17:1-2 & 7 God said, *1When Abram was ninety-nine years old, the Lord appeared to him and said, "I am God Almighty; walk before me and be blameless." 2"I will confirm my covenant between me and you and will greatly increase your numbers." 7 "I will establish my covenant as an everlasting covenant between me and you and your descendants after you for the generations to come, to be your God and the God of your descendants after you.* (NIV)

God confirmed His covenant in the lives of Abraham, Isaac, Jacob, Joseph, the children of Israel, David, Solomon, King Jehoshaphat, King Hezekiah, and many others throughout the Bible who trusted in His promises and obeyed His commandments. God promised to abundantly bless the descendants of Abraham who would follow Abraham's example. You've become a descendant of Abraham through your faith in Christ Jesus (Galatians 3:29). God will also confirm His covenant in your life if you'll add faith and patience to His promises (Hebrews 6:12-15).

Read II Corinthians 8:9. *For you are becoming progressively acquainted with and recognizing more strongly and clearly the grace of our Lord Jesus Christ (His kindness, His gracious generosity, His undeserved favor and spiritual blessing), [in] that though He was [so very] rich, yet for your sakes He became [so very] poor, in order that by His poverty you might become enriched (abundantly supplied).* (AMP)

Jesus paid the price for you to become abundantly supplied in every area of your life. God's promises of abundance are part of your inheritance as a child of God. Lack comes from the devil. The Bible says poverty and lack destroy (Proverbs 10:15). Destruction doesn't come from God (John 10:10).

God's plan is to abundantly bless you so you can be a blessing to others. If you don't walk in the promises of God concerning your finances, you won't be able to give generously to promote the gospel of Jesus Christ. Your motive for wanting to be blessed must not be for selfish gain; you must have the heart of a generous giver. The Bible says in Acts 20:35, *remember the words of the Lord Jesus, how he said, It is more blessed to give than to receive.* Jesus paid the price for you to walk in abundance so you can be a blessing to others.

SUMMARY

Remember, lack of knowledge, unbelief and disobedience keep many of God's people from receiving His promises. No matter how many promises He has made, they all find their "yes" answer in Christ Jesus. If you want to partake of the promises of God concerning your health and finances, you must say "Amen, so be it in my life!" If you'll add faith and patience to God's Word, you'll have life in abundance, for God will watch over His Word to perform it in your life!

PERSONAL APPLICATION

Write down three promises God has given you concerning health and healing.

1. _____
   _____
2. _____
   _____
3. _____
   _____

Write down three promises God has given you concerning finances.

1. _____
   _____
2. _____
   _____
3. _____
   _____

Begin to meditate on these six promises and put them in your heart.

How can you receive these promises of God in your life? (Hebrews 6:12)

_____

What two actions does real faith take? What two things will you do when you add real faith to God's promises? (II Corinthians 4:13)

1. _____

2. _____

Add faith to God's promises by confessing them to be true in your life:

- By the stripes of Jesus I am healed.
- God's Word brings health and healing to all my flesh.
- God has forgiven all my sins and healed all my diseases.
- My God shall supply all of my needs according to His riches in glory.
- God is able to make all grace abound toward me so that I have financial abundance and can give abundantly to every good work.
- Thank you Lord for Your wisdom that gives me clever inventions and ideas, for You've given me the power to obtain wealth so that You might establish Your covenant in my life.
- I'm blessed when I come in and I am blessed when I go out. The Lord will command His blessings upon me and will abundantly prosper the works of my hands. I'll be the lender and not the borrower, the head and not the tail. Everyone will see that I'm blessed of the Lord, for I choose to walk in His ways.

What promise did God give you in Mark 11:23 concerning speaking His Word over your life?_____

_____

Continue to speak God's Word over your health and finances. His promise to you is that if you'll confess His Word and not doubt in your heart but believe that what you say will happen, He will watch over His Word and perform it in your life!

God's Promises for Success, the Desires of Your Heart, and Answered Prayer

PURPOSE

To study three areas of your life in which God has given you great and precious promises so that you don't lack knowledge of His perfect plan for you.

OVERVIEW

God has promised success in life when you choose to obey Him and walk in His ways. He has also promised to fulfill the desires of your heart and answer your prayers. God loves you and has revealed His wonderful plan for you in His Word. If you'll put your trust in the promises He has made, He'll watch over His Word to perform it in your life.

DISCUSSION

I. God has given you promises for success in life.

God wants you to be successful in every area of your life. He wants you to have a successful marriage. He wants you to be a successful parent. He wants you to be successful on your job and in your business. He wants you to be prosperous and successful by fulfilling the plan He has for you in every area of your life.

The Bible teaches how you can obtain the success that God wants for you. God has promised this success if you'll follow the instructions He has given in His Word.

Read Joshua 1:8.

What three things does God instruct you to do if you want to be successful through Him?

1. _____

2. _____

3. _____

What does God promise you in this scripture? _____

_____

If you want to be successful in life through God, you must follow His plan for success. His plan includes three steps:

1. Speak His Word. Don't let it depart from your mouth.

2. Meditate upon His Word day and night. Continually fill your mind with the truth of His Word.
3. Walk in obedience to Him.

If you'll do these three things, God promises that you'll make your way prosperous, and you'll have good success.

You can apply this scripture to every area of your life. For example, if you want to be a successful parent, you must:

- Speak God's Word over your children. (See Lesson 4, Part II for God's promises concerning your children.)
- Meditate upon His promises and His counsel regarding your children.
- Obey His Word. Train your children, discipline them, love them, and be a Godly example in their lives.

If you want to have a successful marriage that is blessed by God, you must:

- Speak His Word over your marriage. (See Lesson 4, Part I for God's promises concerning your marriage.)
- Meditate upon His counsel and His promises regarding your marriage.
- Do His Word. Follow His instructions concerning your role as a spouse.

If you want God to bless you on your job or in your business, then you must follow God's plan for success.

- Speak His Word over your job or business.
- Meditate upon His counsel and His promises concerning this area of your life.
- Obey His Word. Be diligent and faithful in your work. (Proverbs 21:5 & 22:29)

As you examine your own life, ask yourself, "Have I been following God's plan for success?" Why or why not?_____

_____

Remember, God says if you'll speak, meditate upon and obey His Word, you'll make your way prosperous and be successful in every area of your life.

Read Psalms 1:1-3. This truth is revealed again in this passage of scripture.

What does the man do who is blessed and prosperous? (verse 2)_____

_____

_____

What does God promise the man who delights in His Word and meditates in it day and night? (verse 3)_____

_____

_____

If you'll delight in obeying the Word of God, and meditate on His promises day and night, He promises that you'll prosper in everything you do.

In Proverbs 16:3 God's Word again establishes the truth that He wants His people to prosper and succeed: *Roll your works upon the Lord [commit and trust them wholly to Him; He will cause your thoughts to become agreeable to His will, and] so shall your plans be established and succeed.* (AMP)

In this scripture, what does His Word promise you when you completely trust in Him?

_____

_____

Many times people follow their own plans and their own ideas without truly acknowledging God. God doesn't promise you success if your plans aren't His plans. On the other hand, Proverbs 16:3 clearly teaches that if you'll completely trust in God, He'll cause your thoughts to become agreeable with His will for your life. Your plans will then become His plans, and they'll be established and will succeed.

God has a special plan and purpose for your life. It's only when you're following that plan that you'll experience true happiness and success. Many times God's people become discouraged and confused because they're trying so hard to figure out His plan for their life. You must realize that if you'll look to God and put your complete trust in Him, He'll fulfill His purpose for you. You don't have to figure it all out. You must trust in His power and ability to bring His plan to pass.

Read Psalm 57:2. *I will cry to God Most High, Who performs on my behalf and rewards me [Who brings to pass His purposes for me and surely completes them]!* (AMP)

What will God do in your life if you'll completely trust in Him?_____

_____

_____

Do you have to be worried that you might miss God's plan? Is it you who brings it to pass, or is it God?

Why can you rest in this truth from God's Word?_____

_____

As you trust in God to bring to pass His plans for you, He'll direct your steps. Read Proverbs 3:5-6.

What three things does God tell you to do?

1. _____

2. _____

3. _____

What does He promise you in this scripture? _____

_____

As you follow God and completely trust Him with your life, He will lead you down the right path.

Read Psalm 37:23. *The steps of a [good] man are directed and established by the Lord when He delights in his way [and He busies Himself with his every step].* (AMP)

According to this scripture, what can you confidently expect God to do in your life?

_____

_____

You can be confident that God will direct and establish your steps when you rest in His ability to bring to pass His plans for your life. This scripture says that when God delights in you, He will busy Himself with your every step.

When does God delight in you? How can you please God? Read Hebrews 11:6.

_____

_____

As you trust in God, He will surround you with favor.

Read Psalm 5:11-12.

What promise is found in verse 12 concerning those who put their trust in God?

_____

_____

God will open the doors for you. He will surround you with His favor. As you rest in Him, He will perform on your behalf and reward you. He will bring to pass His purposes for you and will surely complete them. You'll be a success in life when you put your complete trust in Him.

The Bible clearly teaches that God wants His people to succeed. Read Deuteronomy 28:11-13.

List the many blessings that God will bring into your life if you'll choose to trust and obey His Word._____

_____

_____

God will grant you abundant prosperity in every area of your life. He will bless the work of your hands. His perfect plan for you includes being the lender and not the borrower, being the head and not the tail and being a success and not a failure. As you walk in His wisdom and trust in His Word, He promises that you'll make your way prosperous and you'll have good success! Psalm 35:27 says that God takes pleasure in the prosperity of His people!

II. God has given you promises for the desires of your heart.

What are the desires of your heart concerning your spouse?_____

_____

_____

_____

What are the desires of your heart concerning your children?_____

_____

_____

_____

What are the desires of your heart for yourself?_____

_____

_____

_____

Read Psalm 37:4-5.

In verse 4, what promise does God give you concerning the desires of your heart?

_____

_____

Look at verse 5. This scripture says that God will bring your desires to pass. What must you do in order to receive God's promise?

Read Psalm 145:18-19.

What does God promise you in verse 19? What is the condition of His promise?

_____

_____

Read Proverbs 10:24.

What truth is found in this scripture? _____

_____

Ephesians 3:20 says *Now to Him Who, by (in consequence of) the [action of His] power that is at work within us, is able to [carry out His purpose and] do superabundantly, far over and above all that we [dare] ask or think [infinitely beyond our highest prayers, desires, thoughts, hopes, or dreams].* (AMP)

Is God able to bring your desires to pass? What truth is found in this verse? Rewrite this scripture in personalized form. _____

_____

_____

_____

_____

Do these scriptures convince you that your Heavenly Father will fulfill the desires of your heart? How do they strengthen your trust in God?_____

_____

III. God has given you promises for answered prayer.

God promises in His Word that He will answer your prayers. There is, however, a condition to His promise. The Bible reveals which prayers God has promised to answer.

Read I John 5: 14-15.

When can you have confidence that God will hear and answer your prayers? What is the condition to His promise? (verse 14)_____

_____

According to this scripture, God promises to answer your prayers when you pray according to His will. Where can you find His will for your life?_____

_____

If you were unable to know God's will, then you could never have confidence that He would answer your prayers. However, God has revealed His will to you through His Word. He has shown you what He wants for every area of your life through the many promises He has made in His Word.

For example it's God's will that:

- you walk in health and are healed of every sickness (III John 2; Psalm 103:3; Proverbs 4:20-22).
- you walk in abundance so you can give to others and promote the gospel of Jesus Christ (Phillipians 4:19; II Corinthians 9:6-15).
- you prosper and are successful (Psalm 1:1-3; Joshua 1:8).
- your unsaved family receives salvation (II Peter 3:9; I Timothy 2:4).
- your children follow after Him, obey His Word, and have peace (Isaiah 54:13; Isaiah 44:3-5).
- a husband loves his wife like Christ loves the Church and a wife respects, loves, and admires her husband (Ephesians 5:25,28; Colossians 3:19; I Peter 3:1-2; Titus 2:4).
- His people grow spiritually (Colossians 1:9-12; Ephesians 3:16-20).
- your heart's desire is fulfilled (Psalm 37:4; Psalm 145:19; Proverbs 10:24).
- you be delivered out of every problem or trouble you may face (Psalm 34:17-19; Psalm 37:39-40).
- you be protected from harm (Psalm 91).
- His plan and purpose for your life be fulfilled (Psalm 57:2).
- everything which concerns you be perfected (Psalm 138:8 [AMP]; I Peter 5:7).

In God's Word there is an answer to every problem you face. When you base your prayers on a promise of God, you're praying according to His will. You can pray with confidence when you know what He has promised concerning your situation. As you pray in agreement with His Word and put your trust in His faithfulness, He will never fail to answer your prayer. He will watch over His Word to perform it in your life. If you want to have a successful prayer life, then you must always come to Him on the authority of His Word.

Isaiah 62:6 says: *You who [are His servant and by your prayers] put the Lord in remembrance [of His promises].* (AMP) Therefore, when you ask God for something in prayer, you must always come on the basis of what He has promised you. The Bible teaches that when you pray, you're to remind God of His promises.

When you come to God in prayer, do three things:

1. Know exactly what you need. What is it that you need or want God to do? Present your request to Him. Read Phillipians 4:6.
2. Find a scripture or a promise in His Word that reveals His will concerning your situation. Then when you pray, remind Him of what He has promised you. His promise will give you strength to stand strong until your answer comes.
3. Believe and be confident that He has heard and answered your prayer even before you see it come to pass in the natural.

Read Mark 11:24. *For this reason I am telling you, whatever you ask for in prayer, believe (trust and be confident) that it is granted to you, and you will [get it].* (AMP)

According to this scripture, what must you do in order to receive the answer to your prayer?

_____

_____

In this scripture, Jesus teaches you how to receive answers to your prayers. He says to be confident that your prayer is answered before you actually see it come to pass. In other words, you must claim God's promise to be so in your life no matter what circumstances look like, and then you'll receive the answer to your prayer.

Read Matthew 21:22. *And whatever you ask for in prayer, having faith and [really] believing, you will receive.* (AMP)

What's the condition of this promise? Personalize this scripture. _____

_____

_____

You can't just hope that God will answer your prayer. You must be confident and really believe that you have what you asked of Him. This is the kind of prayer that God promises to answer.

Read John 15:7.

Who will receive the answers to their prayers? What is the condition of this promise?

_____

_____

How can you know you're abiding in Christ? Read I John 3:24._____

_____

_____

This scripture teaches that when you live a life of obedience, you're abiding in Christ. God's Word will abide in your heart as you meditate upon it day and night. The Bible says when you abide in Christ and His Word abides in you, you can ask what you will and it shall be done!

Read I John 3:21-23.

Why does God answer your prayers? (verse 22) _____

_____

What two things please God? (verse 23)_____

_____

Read John 16:23-24.

According to verse 24, why does God want to answer your prayers?_____

_____

If you're experiencing difficulty receiving answers to your prayers, you mustn't doubt God's faithfulness. Examine your own life to see if there are any attitudes or actions hindering you from receiving His promise.

What attitudes and actions will keep you from receiving answers to your prayers? The answer can be found in God's Word.

James 1:6-7_____

James 4:2-3_____

Psalm 66:18_____

Mark 11:25_____

I Peter 3:7_____

You must keep your heart pure before God in order to have confidence before Him in prayer. I John 3:21 says that if your heart doesn't condemn you, you can have confidence that God will answer your prayers. As you trust in God and obey His Word, your prayers will do a powerful work in your life and in the lives of others. The Bible says in James 5:16 *The earnest (heartfelt, continued) prayer of a righteous man makes tremendous power available [dynamic in its working].* (AMP)

SUMMARY

God's promises of success in life and answered prayer belong to you as His child. You can claim them to be true in your life. He has also promised to fulfill the desires of your heart. According to II Corinthians 1:20, all of these promises find their "Yes" answer in Christ Jesus; therefore, you can confidently respond to God's promises by saying "Amen, so be it in my life!" Remember, God is faithful to those who will trust and obey His Word. When you put your complete confidence in Him, you'll be a living testimony that God is faithful to His promises.

PERSONAL APPLICATION

Take time to meditate on three promises that you learned in this lesson. God's Word will abide in your heart as you think about His promises. The Bible teaches that the amount of thought and study you give to the truth you hear will determine the amount of revelation knowledge and spiritual strength you receive from God's Word (Mark 4:24).

MEMORIZE

Memorize and meditate upon the following scriptures:

- Joshua 1:8: *Do not let this Book of the Law depart from your mouth; meditate on it day and night, so that you may be careful to do everything written in it. Then you will be prosperous and successful.* (NIV)

- Psalm 37:4: *Delight yourself in the Lord and he will give you the desires of your heart.* (NIV)

- I John 5:14-15: *14This is the confidence we have in approaching God: that if we ask anything according to his will, he hears us. 15And if we know that he hears us — whatever we ask — we know that we have what we asked of him.* (NIV)

REVIEW QUESTIONS

1. What three things must you do to follow God's plan for success? (Joshua 1:8)
   a. _____
   b. _____
   c. _____

2. What has God promised concerning the desires of your heart?_____
   _____

3. When can you have confidence that God will hear and answer your prayers? (I John 5:14-15)_____
   _____

4. Where can you find God's will for your life?_____
   _____

5. What are some attitudes and actions that will keep you from receiving answers to your prayers?_____
   _____
   _____
   _____

You learned in this lesson to do three things when you come to God in prayer. Apply these three steps to your own life. Two personal application sheets have been given in case there is more than one area of your life in which you have a need or desire for God to do a work.

SITUATION #1

1. What do you need or desire God to do in your life? Make your request known to Him.

   _____

   _____

   _____

   _____

2. Find 3-5 scriptures or promises in God's Word that reveal His will concerning this area of your life. Use the promises from the Bible study or search for new ones. When you pray according to God's will, He promises that He will hear and answer (I John 5:14-15).

   a. _____

   _____

   b. _____

   _____

   c. _____

   _____

   d. _____

   _____

   e. _____

   _____

   As you pray, remind God of His promises.

3. Pray and ask God to fulfill His will in your life. Believe and be confident that He has answered your prayer, and you'll receive what He has promised. Continually thank Him that He has answered your prayer before you see it come to pass in the natural.

   Date on which you prayed: _____

   Date prayer was answered: _____

If you'll add faith and patience to God's promises, you'll receive all He has planned for you. When you put your trust in Him, you'll never be disappointed.

Progress report: If your prayer has to do with someone's spiritual growth, or God performing His will in your marriage, write down the changes you see taking place as God performs His Word in your life. _____

_____

_____

_____

_____

SITUATION #2

1. What do you need or desire God to do in your life? Make your request known to Him.

   _____

   _____

   _____

   _____

2. Find 3-5 scriptures or promises in God's Word that reveal His will concerning this area of your life. Use the promises from the Bible study or search for new ones. When you pray according to God's will, He promises that He will hear and answer (I John 5:14-15).

   a. _____

   _____

   b. _____

   _____

   c. _____

   _____

   d. _____

   _____

   e. _____

   _____

   As you pray, remind God of His promises.

3. Pray and ask God to fulfill His will in your life. Believe and be confident that He has answered your prayer, and you'll receive what He has promised. Continually thank Him that He has answered your prayer before you see it come to pass in the natural.

   Date on which you prayed: _____

   Date prayer was answered: _____

If you'll add faith and patience to God's promises, you'll receive all He has planned for you. When you put your trust in Him, you'll never be disappointed.

Progress report: If your prayer has to do with someone's spiritual growth, or God performing His will in your marriage, write down the changes you see taking place as God performs His Word in your life. _____

_____

_____

_____

_____

Lesson 8
What Does it Mean to Put Your Trust in God's Promises?

PURPOSE

To study the definition of the word "trust" and thereby gain a greater understanding of what it means to really put your trust in God.

OVERVIEW

You learned previously that unbelief and lack of knowledge keep many of God's people from receiving all they've been promised. In the previous lessons you overcame lack of knowledge by learning some of the many promises God has given you in His Word. However, even though you know God's promises, if you don't put your trust in them, they won't benefit your life. It's important to understand what it means to really put your trust in the promises of God. In order to do this, you'll study four definitions of the word "trust." Often, people think they're trusting God when they actually don't understand what it means to trust. When you complete this lesson, you'll know whether or not you've really put your trust in what God has promised. Only when you trust in God's Word will you receive all that He has planned for you.

DISCUSSION

Many verses throughout the Bible show us the importance of trusting God.

Psalm 18:30: *As for God, His way is perfect! The word of the Lord is tested and tried; He is a shield to all those who take refuge and put their **trust** in Him.* (AMP)

Psalm 28:7: *The Lord is my Strength and my [impenetrable] Shield; my heart **trusts** in, relies on, and confidently leans on Him, and I am helped.* (AMP)

Psalm 84:12: *O Lord of hosts, blessed (happy, fortunate, to be envied) is the man who **trusts** in you.* (AMP)

Psalm 37:39-40: *But the salvation of the [consistently] righteous is of the Lord; He is their Refuge and secure Stronghold in the time of trouble. And the Lord helps them and delivers them; He delivers them from the wicked and saves them, because they **trust** and take refuge in Him.* (AMP)

Hebrews 6:12: *Behaving as do those who through faith (...**absolute trust and confidence** in His power, wisdom, and goodness) and by practice of patient endurance and waiting are [now] inheriting the promises.* (AMP)

These scriptures clearly show some of the blessings that come from putting your complete trust in God.

According to these scriptures, what does God promise those who put their trust in Him?

_____

_____

_____

_____

God is faithful to fulfill His promises in the lives of His people who choose to put their absolute trust in Him. You'll either trust in God and receive His promises, or you'll doubt His Word and fail to receive His perfect plan for you.

Read James 1:6-7. *6But when he asks, he must believe and not doubt, because he who doubts is like a wave of the sea, blown and tossed by the wind. 7That man should not think he will receive any-thing from the Lord.* (NIV)

What truth is found in these verses concerning those who doubt God's promises?

_____

_____

Doubt is the opposite of trust. The Bible teaches that doubt will keep you from receiving anything from God, so knowing whether or not you're really trusting in God's Word is extremely important.

We'll study four definitions of the word "trust" so you can examine yourself to see if you've really put your complete trust in His promises.

According to the *Thorndike Dictionary*:

1. **"Trust" means "to have a firm belief in the honesty, truthfulness and power of a person."**

According to this definition, then, if you're trusting in what God has promised, you have a firm belief in the truthfulness of His Word. You believe that He would never lie about what He has promised. You have a firm belief that He is honest and trustworthy; you put your complete confidence in His Word.

Example: What has God promised you? Look back over some of the promises you learned about in lessons 4-7. As you think about each scripture, ask yourself, "Do I have a firm belief in the honesty, truthfulness and power of God to fulfill these promises in my life?"

Recall God's promises concerning your marriage. Do you have a firm belief in the truthfulness and power of God to accomplish His perfect will for your marriage? (I John 5:14-15; Proverbs 31:10-31)

Psalm 37:4 says: *Delight yourself also in the Lord, and He will give you the desires and secret petitions of your heart.* (AMP)

Look back over the desires of your heart that you wrote in Lesson 7. Do you firmly believe that God will bring these desires to pass?_____

Proverbs 22:6 says: *Train up a child in the way he should go, and when he is old, he will not depart from it.* (KJV)

Do you have a firm belief in the truthfulness of this scripture? Do you have such confidence in God's Word that you firmly believe your children won't depart from God?_____

Job 22:30 says: *He will even deliver the one [for whom you intercede] who is not innocent; yes, he will be delivered through the cleanness of your hands.* (AMP)

Think about your unsaved family members. Do you have a firm belief in God's honesty, truthfulness and power to fulfill this promise in their lives? Do you firmly believe that God will deliver them out of the control of darkness and transfer them into the kingdom of His Son?_____

Psalm 91:9-11 says: *9Because you have made the Lord your refuge, And the Most High your dwelling place, 10There shall no evil befall you, nor any plague or calamity come near your tent. 11For He will give His angels [especial] charge over you to accompany and defend and preserve you in all your ways.* (AMP)

Do you have a firm belief that no evil, disease or calamity will come near your home? Do you firmly believe that God has given His angels special charge over you to keep you from all harm?_____

Psalm 34:17 & 19 say, *17The righteous cry out, and the Lord hears them; He delivers them from all their troubles....19A righteous man may have many troubles, but the Lord delivers him from them all.* (NIV)

Do you have a firm belief that God will deliver you from every problem you face?

_____

Read Numbers 23:19: *God is not a man, that he should lie, nor a son of man, that he should change his mind. Does he speak and then not act? Does he promise and not fulfill?* (NIV)

Explain what this scripture tells you about God's truthfulness. Would God ever lie to you about what He has promised?_____

_____

Hasn't God said that He will fulfill the desires of your heart? Won't He do it? Hasn't He purposed to deliver those you intercede for? Won't He make it good?

Hasn't God said, "If you trust Me, I will command my angels to protect you"? Won't He do it? Hasn't He purposed to bless you so you can be a blessing? Won't He make it good?

Hasn't God said that He will deliver you from all your troubles? Won't He do it? Hasn't He purposed to answer your prayers? Won't He make it good?

God is honest, and His Word is trustworthy. He watches over His Word to perform it in the lives of those who put their trust in what He has promised.

Examine yourself: Do you have a firm belief in the honesty and truthfulness of God's Word? Do you firmly believe that He will fulfill His promises in your life?

_____

If you can answer "Yes" to these questions, then you've put your trust in God.

2. "Trust" means "to have faith; to believe; depend on."

According to this definition, if you're really trusting in God's promises, you'll depend on Him to perform His Word in your life. You'll add faith to the promises found in His Word.

According to the Moffett translation of Hebrews 11:1, "faith" means "to be *confident* of what we hope for and *convinced* of what we cannot see."

Think of three or four promises found in God's Word that you hope will come to pass in your life. In which promises have you put your hope?

_____

_____

_____

_____

_____

When you're truly trusting in God's promises, you're **confident** that what you hope for will become a reality in your life.

Read II Corinthians 4:13. *It is written: "I believed; therefore I have spoken." With that same spirit of faith we also believe and therefore speak.* (NIV)

What does it mean to add faith to God's promises? What are the two parts of faith?

_____

_____

Believing in your heart + confessing with your mouth = FAITH!

If you've really put your trust in God, then you'll boldly speak in agreement with what He has promised.

In Hebrews 11:1 the *Amplified Bible* says *faith perceives as real fact what is not revealed to the senses.* In other words, when you put your absolute trust in the promises of God, you see them as a fact in your life. You're convinced of the reality of God's promises in the face of physical evidence to the contrary. You're confident that what He has promised **will** happen, even though you might be facing circumstances that make the fulfillment of His promises seem impossible.

For example:

- You look past your circumstances and see through the eyes of faith. Proverbs 29:18 says that without a vision, God's people perish. If you're truly trusting in God's promise, you visualize them already fulfilled in your life no matter what it looks like in the natural.

- You have a vision of your unsaved family serving God (Acts 16:31). Your faith perceives this as **real fact**!

- You have a vision of God's will coming to pass in your marriage (Ephesians 5:22-33; I John 5:14-15).

- You have a vision of the desires of your heart coming to pass (Psalm 37:4-5).

- You envision yourself being so abundantly blessed that you're able to give generously to every good work (II Corinthians 9:6-11).

- You envision your business being abundantly prosperous (Deuteronomy 30:8-9).

- You envision yourself overflowing in the blessings of God (Deuteronomy 28:1-13). Your faith perceives this as **real fact**!

Even if your natural circumstances tell you that none of this is true, when you trust God, you're so convinced that His promise will come to pass it's as though it's already done. You have the title deed to God's promise; you're just waiting for the delivery.

Examine yourself: Are you confident of what you hope for? Are you convinced that what God has promised, He will perform in your life?_____

Do you have a vision of God's promises becoming reality?_____

If you can answer "Yes" to these questions, then you've put your trust in God.

3. "Trust" means "a confident expectation."

If you're truly trusting in God's promises, you confidently expect Him to fulfill them in your life. If you're just hoping something will happen, you aren't to the point of fully trusting.

If you're really trusting in the promises of God:

- You confidently expect God to perform His will in your marriage.

- You are confident that your children will be mighty and blessed upon the earth and you're certain that they won't depart from serving God (Psalm 112:1-2).

- You confidently expect God to fulfill the desires of your heart (Psalm 145:19).

- You are confident that God's perfect plan for your life will come to pass (Psalm 57:2).

- You are confident that God will command His angels to protect you and that He will keep you from harm (Psalm 91:9-11).

- You know with confidence that God will command His blessings upon you and will surround you with His favor because you expect Him to do what He has promised (Psalm 5:11-12).

Examine yourself: Are you confident that God will fulfill His promises in your life? Do you **expect** Him to perform what He has promised? _____

_____

_____

If you can answer "Yes" to these questions, then you've put your trust in God.

4. "Trust" means "something committed to one's care."

According to this definition, when you trust God, you give Him the responsibility of taking care of all your concerns.

Read I Peter 5:7. *Casting the whole of your care [all your anxieties, all your worries, all your concerns, once and for all] on Him, for He cares for you affectionately and cares about you watchfully.* (AMP)

According to this scripture, what does God want you to do with what you're worried or concerned about?_____

_____

Are you really trusting God if you're worried about something?_____

What concerns do you have that you haven't given to God?_____

_____

According to this scripture, why does God want you to give Him your cares?_____

_____

_____

Psalm 138:8 says: *The Lord will perfect that which concerns me.* (AMP)

According to this scripture, when you cast your cares on God, what can you be confident of?

_____

_____

God cares about everything that concerns you. There isn't one area of your life that He doesn't care about. He wants you to cast your cares on Him because He cares about you affectionately. When you cast your cares on God, He will perfect that which concerns you.

You may ask, "How do I cast my care on God?"

When you truly cast your care on God, you give Him your problem, and He gives you His promise. You replace your thoughts of anxiety, worry and concern with thoughts of His promises. The only way you can cast your care on God is if you know what He has promised concerning your situation. As you keep your mind filled with His promises and put your trust in Him, you'll have His perfect peace.

For example:

If you're worrying about what God's plan or purpose is for your life, and about what direction you should take, here's how you cast this care on Him:

Search His Word for a promise in which you can put your trust, one on which you can focus. Give your concern or care to God and begin to meditate on His promises:

- God will perform on my behalf and reward me. He will bring His purposes to pass for me and will surely complete them (Psalm 57:2).

- God has plans to prosper me and to give me hope for my future (Jeremiah 29:11).
- God will bring His purpose to pass for me and will do exceedingly above my highest prayers, desires, thoughts, hopes, or dreams (Ephesians 3:20).
- I will trust in the Lord with all my heart and lean not to my own understanding. In all my ways I will acknowledge Him, and He will direct my paths (Proverbs 3:5-6).

When you cast your care about this situation on God, you'll fill your mind and heart with God's promises. You'll then have God's perfect peace, knowing that He has something wonderful in store for your life, and you'll be confident that He will bring it to pass.

You can't think about the problem and the promise at the same time. One will give you peace (God's promise), the other will give you worry and fear (your concern).

Apply this truth to a situation in your life. What have you been worried about?

_____

_____

_____

What has God promised you concerning this situation?

_____

_____

_____

Now you can know whether you're truly trusting in God by what you fill your mind with — the promise or the problem. Isaiah 26:3-4 reveals that those who keep their mind on God will be able to trust Him in every situation.

Examine yourself: Have you cast your care on God? Have you given Him the responsibility of taking care of your concerns? Are you filling your heart and mind with His promises concerning your situation?

If you can answer "Yes" to these questions, then you have put your trust in God.

The Bible reveals that when you're truly putting your trust in God, your heart and mind will have perfect peace.

Read Isaiah 26:3-4. *3You will guard him and keep him in perfect and constant peace whose mind is stayed on You, because he commits himself to You, leans on You and hopes confidently in You. 4So trust in the Lord — commit yourself to Him, lean on Him, hope confidently in Him — for ever; for the Lord God is an everlasting rock — the Rock of ages.* (AMP)

According to verse 3, what is the characteristic of a person who completely trusts God concerning their situation?_____

"Peace" is defined as "freedom from disturbing thoughts or emotions. When you've put your trust in God, you won't worry about or be fearful of any situation in your life.

A person who has perfect peace keeps his mind or thoughts on what? (verse 3)

_____

If you continue to concentrate on your problem, you'll fill your heart with doubt. You'll be full of worry and fear concerning your situation. When you keep your mind focused on God and meditate on His promises, you'll fill your heart with faith and you'll have God's perfect peace.

Read Phillipians 4:6-7: *6Don't worry about anything; instead, pray about everything; tell God your needs and don't forget to thank him for his answers. 7If you do this you will experience God's peace, which is far more wonderful than the human mind can understand. His peace will keep your thoughts and your hearts quiet and at rest as you trust in Christ Jesus.* (TLB)

What should you do when a situation arises that you're tempted to be worried or concerned about?_____

_____

What characteristic will be present in your life as you trust in God?_____

_____

Read Phillipians 4:8. *Finally, brothers, whatever is true, whatever is noble, whatever is right, whatever is pure, whatever is lovely, whatever is admirable — if anything is excellent or praiseworthy — think about such things.* (NIV)

If you want God's peace, with what should you fill your mind?_____

_____

_____

When you fill your mind with God's Word, you'll have His perfect peace.

Examine yourself: Do you have perfect peace concerning your situation?_____

Do you keep your mind on God and meditate on His promises when you're facing difficult circumstances?_____

If you can answer "Yes" to this question, then you've put your trust in God.

SUMMARY

When you put your trust in God, you'll receive all He has promised. This is why it's so important to examine yourself to see if you're really trusting in the promises He has made in His Word. In this lesson you studied four definitions of the word "trust." You learned that when you're really trusting in the promises of God:

- You'll have a **firm belief in the honesty, truthfulness and power** of God to fulfill His promises in your life.
- You're **confident** of what you hope for and *convinced* of what you can't see.
- You have a vision of His promises becoming a reality in your life and you confidently speak what you believe.
- You **confidently expect** God to do what He has promised.

- You **commit all of your cares and concerns** into God's hands. You cast your cares on Him and replace them with His promise.
- You won't be worried or concerned; you'll have God's **perfect peace**.

PERSONAL APPLICATION

Examine yourself to see if you're really trusting God to fulfill the promises that you wrote down in the Personal Application in Lesson 7.

SELF EXAMINATION

Look back to Lesson 7's Personal Application. On what scriptures or promises are your prayers based?
Situation # 1.

a. _____
_____

b. _____
_____

c. _____
_____

d. _____
_____

e. _____
_____

Have you memorized these Scriptures? Are you filling your heart with God's Word by meditating on them every day?_____

Try to quote these scriptures from memory. If you haven't memorized them, take time to memorize God's Word so you can meditate on these scriptures and strengthen your trust in Him. If you don't know these scriptures, how can you replace your thoughts of doubt or worry with His promises?

Are you really trusting God to fulfill these promises in your life?

1. Do you have a firm belief in the honesty, truthfulness and power of God to bring to pass these promises in your life?_____

2. Do you confidently expect God to perform His Word in your life? Do you know that God will perform what He has promised you?_____

3. Are you confident of what you hope for? _____

4. Do you have a vision of these promises of God becoming a reality in your life?
_____

5. Have you been confidently claiming these promises to be true in your life?_____

6. Do you fill your mind with the promise and not the problem? Have you cast your care on God and replaced your thoughts of worry and concern with thoughts of His promises?_____

7. Do you have God's perfect peace?_____

If you answered "Yes" to all of these questions, then you've put your complete trust in God concerning this area of your life. You're in a position to receive all He has promised you, and you're doing your part by adding faith to His promises. Now all you have to do is be patient and wait on Him to manifest His promise in your life.

If you couldn't honestly answer "Yes" to all these questions, don't become discouraged. God has revealed in His Word the process that can bring you to this place of trust. You'll examine this process in lesson 10. If you'll follow God's instructions, you'll be able to trust Him in every situation.

It's important to look through the eyes of faith and see the promise already fulfilled. It should be so real to you that you see it as already accomplished. It's like ordering a package and knowing that it's on its way. You're just waiting for the delivery. When your package arrives, how will it make a difference in your life?

The Bible says that without a vision, God's people perish (Proverbs 29:18). Write your vision down. What will be present in your life when God fulfills His promises?

Date_____

Your vision of the answer to your prayer:

_____
_____
_____
_____
_____
_____
_____
_____
_____
_____

Habakkuk 2:2-3 says: *And the Lord answered me and said, Write the vision and engrave it so plainly upon tablets that everyone who passes may [be able to] read [it easily and quickly] as he hastens by. For the vision is yet for an appointed time and it hastens to the end [fulfillment]; it will not deceive or disappoint. Though it tarry, wait [earnestly] for it, because it will surely come; it will not be behindhand on its appointed day.* (AMP)

Date vision became reality:_____

Situation #2.

a. _____

_____

b. _____

_____

c. _____

_____

d. _____

_____

e. _____

_____

Have you memorized these scriptures? Are you filling your heart with God's Word by meditating on them every day?_____

Try to quote these scriptures from memory. If you haven't memorized them, take time to memorize God's Word so you can meditate on these scriptures and strengthen your trust in Him. If you don't know these scriptures, how can you replace your thoughts of doubt or worry with His promises?

Are you really trusting God to fulfill these promises in your life?

1. Do you have a firm belief in the honesty, truthfulness and power of God to bring to pass these promises in your life?_____

2. Do you confidently expect God to perform His Word in your life? Do you know that God will perform what He has promised you?_____

3. Are you confident of what you hope for? _____

4. Do you have a vision of these promises of God becoming a reality in your life?

_____

5. Have you been confidently claiming these promises to be true in your life?_____

_____

6. Do you fill your mind with the promise and not the problem? Have you cast your care on God and replaced your thoughts of worry and concern with thoughts of His promises?_____

7. Do you have God's perfect peace? _____

If you answered "Yes" to all of these questions, then you've put your complete trust in God concerning this area of your life. You're in a position to receive all He has promised you, and you're doing your part by adding faith to His promises. Now all you have to do is be patient and wait on Him to manifest His promise in your life.

If you couldn't honestly answer "Yes" to all these questions, don't become discouraged. God has revealed in His Word the process that can bring you to this place of trust. You'll examine this process in lesson 10. If you'll follow God's instructions, you'll be able to trust Him in every situation.

It's important to look through the eyes of faith and see the promise already fulfilled. It should be so real to you that you see it as already accomplished. It's like ordering a package and knowing that it's on its way. You're just waiting for the delivery. When your package arrives, how will it make a difference in your life?

The Bible says that without a vision, God's people perish (Proverbs 29:18). Write your vision down. What will be present in your life when God fulfills His promises?

Date_____

Your vision of the answer to your prayer:

_____

_____

_____

_____

_____

_____

_____

_____

_____

_____

Habakkuk 2:2-3 says: *And the Lord answered me and said, Write the vision and engrave it so plainly upon tablets that everyone who passes may [be able to] read [it easily and quickly] as he hastens by. For the vision is yet for an appointed time and it hastens to the end [fulfillment]; it will not deceive or disappoint. Though it tarry, wait [earnestly] for it, because it will surely come; it will not be behindhand on its appointed day.* (AMP)

Date vision became reality:_____

Lesson 9
Trusting God Produces Obedience

PURPOSE

To realize that when you've really put your trust in God, you'll walk in obedience to His Word. To learn that as you depend on God's grace, He will create in you the desire and ability to live a life of obedience.

OVERVIEW

You've learned that in order to inherit God's promises, you must put your trust in His Word. The Bible teaches that when you put your trust in God, you'll follow His counsel. You'll be confident that by obeying Him, you'll receive His abundant blessings in your life. There is a condition to every promise He has made. The doer of God's Word is the one who will receive the promises. When you put your trust in Him, His grace will create in you the desire and ability to live a life that pleases Him.

DISCUSSION

In the Word of God, you can find the answer to every problem you face. God has given you a promise for every problem. With each of His promises, you have a part to play; there is an action that God wants you to take. When you act upon His Word, you're trusting in the counsel of God. He's the greatest marriage counselor, family counselor, and financial advisor you'll ever find. If you'll act upon His wisdom, you'll walk in abundant life. When you obey Him, you're proving that you're completely trusting Him with every area of your life.

I. Your actions make your faith complete.

Read James 2:20-22: 20*Fool! When will you learn that "believing" is useless without doing what God wants you to? Faith that does not result in good deeds is not real faith. 21Don't you remember that even our father Abraham was declared good because of what he did, when he was **willing to obey God**, even if it meant offering his son Isaac to die on the alter? 22You see, he was **trusting God so much** that he was willing to do whatever God told him to; his faith was made complete by what he did, by his actions, his good deeds.* (TLB)

What does God want you to learn in verse 20?_____

_____

How do you know Abraham was truly trusting God? (verse 22)_____

_____

_____

According to Abraham's example, how can you know if you're truly trusting God with every situation in your life?_____

_____

How was Abraham's faith made complete? How can your faith be made complete?

_____

_____

Your trust in God is made complete by your actions. You're completely trusting God when you confidently expect Him to keep His promise, and when you're willing to obey His Word.

If you trust in the wisdom of God, then you'll apply His Word to every area of your life. When you're sick, you trust in the doctor's wisdom to tell you what to do to feel better. Your trust is apparent when you go home and immediately begin doing what the doctor has instructed. Many times, however, we go to God with a problem (marriage, finances, relationships, rebellious children, unsaved loved ones, businesses, etc.), but we don't trust Him enough to do what His Word says. We don't immediately begin applying His wisdom to our situation (often reasoning it away), so we never truly allow God to help us.

Read Matthew 7:24-27. *24So everyone who hears these words of Mine and acts upon them [obeying them] will be like a sensible (prudent, practical, wise) man who built his house upon the rock. 25And the rain fell and the floods came and the winds blew and beat against that house; yet it did not fall, because it had been founded on the rock. 26And everyone who hears these words of Mine and does not do them will be like a stupid (foolish) man who built his house upon the sand. 27And the rain fell and the floods came and the winds blew and beat against that house, and it fell—and great and complete was the fall of it.* (AMP)

What does Jesus call the man who hears the Word of God and chooses to obey it? (verse 24)

_____

Explain what you believe Jesus means by saying "his house was built on a rock." Read Proverbs 24:3-4. _____

_____

_____

How did the trials of life affect the man who obeyed God's Word? (verse 25)

_____

_____

What does Jesus call the man who hears the Word of God, but doesn't choose to trust in it by acting on what he has heard? (verse 26)_____

_____

Explain what you think Jesus meant when he said "his house was built on sand."

_____

_____

What happened to the man who heard the Word of God but chose not to do it? How did the trials of life affect him? (verse 27)_____

_____

_____

For example:

Two men both hear the Word of God which says *love one another as I have loved you* (John 15: 12). I Corinthians 13:4-7 gives a clear understanding of what it means to love one another.

The Doer of God's Word	The Hearer Only
• quickly forgives when wronged	• holds unforgiveness and resentment in his heart
• quickly asks forgiveness	• justifies his sin when he fails
• gives to those in need, has a giving heart	• sees someone in need but isn't willing to sacrifice to help
• isn't offended when wronged	• holds grudges against anyone who hurts him
• is patient and kind	• is impatient and harsh
• is happy when others are blessed	• is full of envy and jealousy when someone else is blessed
• is humble before God, knowing he is only worthy of God's blessings because of Jesus	• takes pride in all his works; thinks he deserves God's blessings because of something he has done
• believes the best of every person	• judges and criticizes people
• puts others before himself	• is selfish; thinks only about himself

In Philippians 4:6-8 both men hear the Word of God say, "Do not worry about anything but pray and thank God for what you need." Verse 8 instructs you to fix your mind on God's Word.

The Doer of God's Word	The Hearer Only
• rests knowing God is faithful; has God's perfect peace concerning his situation.	• worries and frets over his situation; doesn't have God's perfect peace.
• sees God's promise, simply believes it and thanks God for bringing it to pass in his life	• sees God's promise and reasons it away; is full of fear and doubt
• keeps his mind focused on God's promise; believes that nothing is impossible with God.	• keeps his mind on his circumstances; believes his situation is impossible.

Both men hear the same Word; both have the same trials; but only one comes out victoriously — the one who builds his life on the counsel of God's Word.

The doer of the Word trusts in God's wisdom and counsel. When the trials of life come his way, he stands strong on God's Word. He has his feet planted on the Rock (the living Word of God). He can't be shaken. He comes through every trial victoriously.

The hearer of God's Word says he believes the Word of God, but doesn't act on it. When the trials of life come his way he becomes disappointed and discouraged because his faith is weak. He hasn't built his house on the Rock (the counsel of God's Word), so he doesn't have the strength to stand strong.

Examine your own life: Have you been a doer of God's Word, or have you been a hearer only?

We've all had times when we fell into the category of being a hearer only. The real difference between the doer and the hearer isn't that you do everything perfectly, but that you press toward being everything God wants you to be. When the doer of God's Word falls, he's quick to ask forgiveness. He asks God to help him. The doer turns completely away from anything that isn't pleasing to God. He's quick to change when he sees in God's Word where he has been wrong.

Read James 1:21-25. 21*So get rid of all uncleanness and the rampant outgrowth of wickedness, and in a humble (gentle, modest) spirit receive and welcome the Word which implanted and rooted [in your hearts] contains the power to save your souls. 22But be doers of the Word [obey the message], and not merely listeners to it, betraying yourselves [into deception by reasoning contrary to the Truth]. 23For if any one only listens to the Word without obeying it and being a doer of it, he is like a man who looks carefully at his [own] natural face in the mirror; 24For he thoughtfully observes himself, and then goes off and promptly forgets what he was like. 25But he who looks carefully into the faultless law, the [law] of liberty, and is faithful to it and perseveres in looking into it, being not a heedless listener who forgets but an active doer [who obeys], he shall be blessed in his doing (in his life of obedience).* (AMP)

What does verse 21 tell you to do?_____

_____

Your soul consists of your mind, will and emotions. According to verse 21, when you implant God's Word in your heart, what does it have the power to do?_____

_____

Verse 21 teaches that as you implant God's Word in your heart by meditating upon it day and night, it has the power to heal your mind and emotions.

What does verse 22 say you're doing if you listen to God's Word but choose not to follow it?

_____

_____

Look at an example of what it means to reason contrary to the truth.

In Ephesians 4:32 the Word of God says to forgive. When you choose not to forgive, you give all your reasons why that person doesn't deserve to be forgiven. You give reasons why you can't forgive. But what you're really doing is reasoning contrary to the truth, and deceiving yourself.

In I Peter 5:7 God tells you not to worry or be concerned about any situation. Instead, He tells you to cast all your cares on Him. You may think that your situation is impossible. You might not have confidence that God will perfect that which concerns you. When you think this way, you're deceiving yourself by reasoning contrary to the truth.

According to James 1:23-24, what is the man like who listens to the Word of God but doesn't apply it to his life?_____

_____

_____

When you look into God's Word, He shows you how you can be a good spouse, a godly parent, and a prosperous and successful person. He shows you how to overcome fear and doubt and walk in abundant life. If you choose not to act immediately on God's Word and don't begin to apply His wisdom to your life, you'll forget it. The only way you can keep God's Word in your heart is if you meditate upon it day and night and conform your life to His wisdom.

According to James 1:25, how can you have a life filled with the blessings of God?

_____

_____

_____

Read Proverbs 13:13. *Whoever despises the word and counsel [of God] brings destruction upon himself, but he who [reverently] fears and respects the commandment [of God] is rewarded.* (AMP)

What are you bringing upon yourself when you choose not to obey God?_____

_____

What is the result of living a life of obedience to Him?_____

When you choose not to obey the Word of God concerning any area of your life (your marriage, your children, your finances, your health, your business, etc.), you'll bring destruction upon that area. However, the good news is — if you'll choose to obey God's Word and follow His counsel, you'll overflow in His blessings in every area of your life! You have His Word on it!

Read Deuteronomy 30:15 & 19-20: 15*Look, today I have set before you life and death, depending on whether you obey or disobey.* 19*"I call heaven and earth to witness against you that today I have set before you life and death, blessing or curse. Oh, that you would choose life; that you and your children might live!* 20*Choose to love the Lord your God and to obey him and to cling to him, for he is your life and the length of your days."* (TLB)

What two choices has God given you? What are the consequences of each decision?

1. _____

_____

2. _____

_____

What does God want you to choose?

The Bible makes it very clear that God wants you to receive His blessings; but whether you receive them depends on the choices you make. When you choose to obey God, you choose a life filled with His blessings.

Read Proverbs 28:20. *A faithful man shall abound with blessings.* (KJV)

What does God promise the faithful man?_____

_____

The Bible teaches that when you're faithful to obey God's Word, He will fill your life with His blessings. He will bless you with favor, peace, happiness, protection, health, prosperity, and success. He will bless your marriage, your relationship with your children, and with others.

Look at four examples of a doer of God's Word:

1. If you're trusting God to perform His will in your marriage, you'll love your spouse with God's kind of love. You'll trust Him to help you to be the spouse He wants. (I Corinthians 13:4-7; Ephesians 5:22-23; I Peter 3:1-2)

2. If you're trusting in the promises of God concerning your children, you'll train them according to the counsel of God's Word. You'll search His Word for wisdom. You'll humbly receive His Word and you'll be quick to change in areas in which you've been wrong. (Proverbs 29:15, 17; Ephesians 6:1-4; Colossians 3:21; Proverbs 13:24; Proverbs 19:18; Proverbs 22:8)

3. If you're really trusting in the promises of God concerning your finances, you'll be a giver. God's Word says that if you give bountifully, you'll reap bountifully (II Corinthians 9:6-11). If you're a giver, you're a doer of God's Word.

4. If you're trusting God concerning your health, you'll take care of the body He gave you (I Corinthians 6:19-20). You'll follow after wisdom by getting proper rest and eating healthy food. You won't over-indulge and eat more than your body needs (Proverbs 28:7). If you neglect wisdom, you'll open the door for sickness to come upon your body (Proverbs 1:23-33). When you're a doer of God's Word, you'll follow after wisdom and rest secure without fear of sickness.

Read James 2:18. *But someone will say [to you then], You [say you] have faith, and I have [good] works. Now you show me your [alleged] faith apart from any [good] works [if you can], and I by [good] works [of obedience] will show you my faith.* (AMP)

What will your life produce when you're truly trusting God?_____

_____

II. In order to live a life obedient to God, you must depend upon His grace.

The *Amplified Bible* gives an accurate translation of the word "grace" according to the meaning of the original Greek text. Second Corinthians 1:12 tells us grace is *(the unmerited favor and merciful kindness by which God, exerting His holy influence upon souls, turns them to Christ, and keeps, strengthens, and increases them in Christian virtues)*. In other words, it was God's grace that influenced your soul and turned you to Christ. With that same grace, God will influence your will and strengthen and increase you in Christian virtues, giving you the power and ability to obey Him. Paul teaches in Philippians 2:12 that you must be careful to do the good things that result from being saved, obeying God with reverence and shrinking from all that might displease him. In verse 13 he goes on to say that you do this *[not in your own strength] for it is God Who is all the while effectually at work in you [energizing and creating in you the power and desire], both to will and to work for His good pleasure and satisfaction and delight.* (AMP)

According to verse 13, do you have to depend on your own ability to obey God? As you trust in God, what will He do on the inside of you?_____

_____

_____

This scripture clearly reveals that you can't obey God through your own strength. When you put your complete trust in Him, He'll be at work in you giving you the power and ability to be a doer of His Word.

When you put your complete trust in God, you not only confidently expect Him to keep His part of the promise, you also depend on His grace to enable you to do your part.

James 4:6 tells us grace is the *power of the Holy Spirit, to meet this evil tendency and all others fully.* (AMP)

Thus, God's grace is the power of the Holy Spirit at work in your life giving you the strength to overcome every evil tendency of your flesh. James also says that God opposes the proud but gives grace to the humble. When you're humble before God, He gives you grace (the power of the Holy Spirit) to be victorious over sin. When you're humble, you realize that you can do nothing good apart from Him, yet, you can do all things through Him (Philippians 4:13). You realize that it's only because of His strength and His ability at work in you that you're able to be a doer of His Word (John 15:4-5).

Read Galatians 5:16-23.

How can you be free from gratifying the desires of your flesh? (verse 16) _____

_____

According to verse 17, what are the two opposing influences on your will?_____

_____

_____

If you allow yourself to be controlled by your flesh, what will your life produce? (verses 19-21)

_____

_____

_____

If you allow yourself to be controlled by the Holy Spirit, what will His presence within you produce? (verses 22-23)_____

_____

_____

How can you live a life that is controlled by the Holy Spirit?

Read Romans 8:4-6: _4In order that the righteous requirements of the law might be fully met in us, who do not live according to the sinful nature but according to the Spirit. 5Those who live according to the sinful nature have their minds set on what that nature desires; but those who live in accordance with the Spirit have their minds set on what the Spirit desires. 6The mind of sinful man is death, but the mind controlled by the Spirit is life and peace._ (NIV)

According to verse 5, what does the person who lives according to his flesh do? Look at verse 6. What is the result of their actions?_____

_____

_____

What does the person who lives according to the Spirit do? According to verse 6, what is the result of their actions?_____

_____

_____

These verses clearly shows how you can live a life that is controlled by the Holy Spirit. When you set your mind on what pleases God, His grace will be at work in you creating the desire and ability to be a doer of His Word. As you meditate on His Word, the Holy Spirit's presence within you will produce the fruit of the Spirit in your life (Psalm 1:1-3). Romans 8:6 says that when your mind is controlled by the Spirit, you'll walk in abundant life and experience God's perfect peace.

Look at the following example of the difference between a Christian who's controlled by the Spirit and one who's controlled by their flesh:

If a person does something that tempts you to become angry and upset, what you fix your mind on determines whether you live your life controlled by the Holy Spirit or whether you live your life controlled by the flesh.

If you live your life controlled by your flesh, you think about how their actions really made you mad; and, therefore, you hold unforgiveness and resentment in your heart toward them.

If you live your life controlled by the Holy Spirit, you set your mind on God's Word which says: _Great peace have they which love thy law: and nothing shall offend them._ (Psalm 119:165, KJV)

As you meditate on this scripture, your spirit overrides your flesh and you have the desire and ability to do what pleases God. You forgive and forget.

You decide whether you're controlled by your flesh or by God's Spirit. If you think about God's Word, this will bring life and peace. If you think about what pleases your carnal nature, you'll be controlled by your flesh; therefore, you'll reap destruction in your life. Choose abundant life and fix your mind on what pleases God.

SUMMARY

Your faith in God is made complete by obeying His Word. You're completely trusting God when you confidently expect Him to keep His promise and when you're willing to obey. You can't depend on your own strength to be a doer of God's Word. Your flesh wars against your spirit and you need God's strength to give you the desire and ability to obey. God sent the Holy Spirit to be your helper and to guide you into all truth. If you'll simply ask Him to help you, He will give you the supernatural ability to do what is pleasing to God. As you fix your mind on the Word of God, His grace will enable you to overcome your flesh and live a life controlled by the Spirit. Complete trust in God is living a life in which you're depending on Him to guide you, show you, and help you be all He wants you to be.

PERSONAL APPLICATION

If you want to receive all God's promises, you must be a doer of His Word. In order to live a life of obedience, you must allow the Holy Spirit to guide and control you. The Bible teaches that when you fix your mind on God's Word, you'll walk in obedience to what the Holy Spirit desires. Begin today to live a life controlled by the Holy Spirit, and set your mind on what pleases God. Fill your mind with His counsel and wisdom, and you won't follow the desires of your flesh.

MEMORIZE

Psalm 119:165: *Great peace have they who love thy law: and nothing shall offend them.* (KJV)

I Corinthians 13:4-7: *4Love is patient, love is kind. It does not envy, it does not boast, it is not proud. 5It is not rude, it is not self-seeking, it is not easily angered, it keeps no record of wrongs. 6Love does not delight in evil but rejoices with the truth. 7It always protects, always trusts, always hopes, always perseveres.* (NIV)

Philippians 4:13: *I can do all things through Christ which strengtheneth me.* (KJV)

Meditate on the following scriptures:

James 1:25: *But he who looks carefully into the faultless law, the [law] of liberty, and is faithful to it and perseveres in looking into it, being not a heedless listener who forgets, but an active doer [who obeys], he shall be blessed in his doing (his life of obedience).* (AMP)

Proverbs 13:13: *Whoever despises the Word and counsel [of God] brings destruction upon himself, but he who [reverently] fears and respects the commandment [of God] is rewarded.* (AMP)

Proverbs 28:20: *A faithful man shall abound with blessings.* (KJV)

Philippians 2:13: *[Not in your own strength] for it is God Who is all the while effectually at work in you [energizing and creating in you the power and desire], both to will and to work for His good pleasure and satisfaction and delight.* (AMP)

REVIEW QUESTIONS

1. What must you do to inherit God's promises? _____
_____

2. If you're truly trusting in God's Word, what will you do? How is your faith made complete? (James 2:20-22) _____
_____
_____

3. If you're faithful to obey God's Word, with what will He bless your life?
_____
_____
_____

4. Do you have to depend on your own ability to obey God? Explain the truth revealed in Philippians 2:13. _____
_____
_____

5. How can you live a life controlled by the Holy Spirit? (Romans 8:5) _____
_____

If you're truly trusting in God's promises, you'll be a doer of His Word. You'll depend on His grace to do a work in you because it's only through His grace that you're able to do what pleases Him.

Look up the scriptures you've been standing on concerning the need or desire you have in your life. Write down the condition of each promise.

Situation #1:
    a. _____
    b. _____
    c. _____
    d. _____
    e. _____

Situation #2:
    a. _____
    b. _____
    c. _____
    d. _____
    e. _____

Examine yourself. Are you being a doer of God's Word? Are you meeting the conditions of God's promises? Are you trusting God so much that you're willing to obey His Word?

PRAYER

Lord, I ask you to create in me the desire and ability to do those things that are pleasing in your sight. I believe I can do all things through Christ who strengthens me. Thank you for sending the Holy Spirit to guide me into all truth and to help me be all that you want me to be. I'm depending on Your grace to strengthen me and help me love others with your unconditional love. I ask You, Lord, to correct me quickly when I fail and lead me in the way that leads to abundant life. In Jesus' name I pray. Amen

Lesson 10

How Can You Strengthen Your Trust in God?

PURPOSE

To learn how to overcome fear and doubt and really put your trust in God. To understand the process that will bring you to a place of complete confidence in His Word.

OVERVIEW

Now that you understand you must trust in God's Word to receive all He has promised, you may need to learn how to grow to this place of trust. Many Christians have trouble putting their complete confidence in God's Word. They allow their problem to look bigger than His promise. God has shown you, in His Word, the process that will bring you to that place of trust no matter what situation you face. If you want to receive all the promises God has given, you must learn how to strengthen your faith. As you study God's Word, you'll learn how to grow to where you can really cast your cares on God and completely trust Him to fulfill the desires of your heart.

DISCUSSION

I. Why do Christians struggle to trust in God's promises?

There are two main reasons some of God's people struggle to put their trust in Him:

1. **Fear**
   * fear of disappointment
   * fear of failure
   * fear of harm

Have you been experiencing some type of fear that has kept you from completely trusting God? Explain. _____

_____

_____

Fear comes from Satan. II Timothy 1:7 says that God hasn't given you the spirit of fear, but of power and of love and a sound mind. If you allow yourself to fear, it will keep you from putting your complete trust in God.

2. **Doubt**

Doubt is the reason some of God's people aren't able to look past their present circumstances and begin to envision His promises coming to pass in their lives. Their present situation prevents them from believing that He will bring to pass His wonderful plan for them. Doubt causes them to exalt their circumstances above the promises of God.

For example: If you were facing financial struggles, doubt would keep you from being able to look past your present circumstances and envision yourself walking in the abundance that God has promised you.

If you were facing difficulty in your marriage, doubt would keep you from being able to look past the attitudes and actions of your spouse and begin to envision them loving you with God's unconditional love.

- Doubt says it's impossible.

- Doubt says will my situation ever change?

- Doubt says will God really fulfill the desires of my heart?

- Faith says nothing is impossible to those who believe.

- Faith says God's Word is able to do a powerful work in my life.

- Faith says God is able to do infinitely beyond my highest prayers, desires, hopes or dreams.

Can you look past your present circumstances and see God bringing your dreams and desires to pass? Do you have a vision of God's perfect plan coming to pass in your life?

What has kept you from having a vision of God's promises coming to pass in a particular area of your life? Think about what has hindered you from trusting God to bring your dreams and desires to pass._____

_____

_____

Fear and doubt are weapons the enemy uses to deceive you. They'll keep you from putting your complete confidence in the power of God's Word to make a difference in your life.

II. The Bible shows how you can overcome fear and doubt and really put your trust in God.

Read Proverbs 22:17-19: 17*Listen (consent and submit) to the words of the wise, and apply your mind to my knowledge;* 18*For it will be pleasant if you keep them in your mind [believing them]; your lips will be accustomed to [confessing] them.* 19*So that your **trust** (belief, reliance, support, and confidence) may be in the Lord.* (AMP)

This scripture shows the process that will bring you to a point where you can put your complete trust in God's Word concerning every area of your life. There are four steps in this passage. The Bible says if you'll choose to do them, you'll then be able to put your complete trust in God and thereby receive all He has promised.

Step 1: "Listen (consent and submit) to the words of the wise."

Listen to, agree with, and submit to God's Word.
- Seek God's Word for the answer to every situation you face.
- Obey whatever God tells you to do.

You may be struggling to really trust God with your marriage, your children, your finances, your spouse, or with fulfilling the plan He has for your life. The first step is to seek His Word for scriptures that show His will for this area of your life. You can't trust God to do something in your life if you don't know His will. Your faith can't go beyond your knowledge of God's will as it is revealed in His Word.

The first thing you must do is ask yourself "What is God's will, and what has He promised me concerning this situation in my life?" Then search His Word for the answer.

What do you need or want God to do in your life?_____
_____
_____
_____
_____

What is God's will and what has He promised concerning this area of your life?
_____
_____
_____
_____

Now that you know God's will and what He has promised, you must fill your mind with the knowledge of His Word.

Step 2: "Apply your mind to My knowledge."

The second step in this passage tells you to fill your mind with the knowledge that God has given you in His Word. Think about what He has promised concerning this area of your life. Fill your mind with the promise, not the problem. Cast down thoughts of worry and doubt, and meditate on the answer.

Read II Corinthians 10:5: *Casting down imaginations, and every high thing that exalteth itself against the knowledge of God, and bringing into captivity every thought to the obedience of Christ.* (KJV)

What does this scripture tell you to do when you have thoughts of worry and doubt concerning your situation?_____
_____

With what must you fill your mind?_____
_____

This scripture teaches you to cast down every thought of fear and doubt and then fill your mind with the truth of God's Word. Another translation tells you to cast down any argument, theory or reasoning contrary to the Word of God. If you continue to think about your problem, your circumstances will overwhelm you and they'll rob you of your faith. On the other hand, if you'll keep your mind focused on what God has promised, your problem will begin to seem small as your confidence in God grows strong!

Romans 12:2 teaches that you must renew your mind to God's Word: *be transformed (changed) by the [entire] renewal of your mind[by its new ideals and its new attitude], so that you may prove [for yourselves] what is the good and acceptable and perfect will of God, even the thing which is good and acceptable and perfect [in His sight for you].* (AMP)

What does this scripture teach that you will prove to yourself when you renew your mind to the knowledge of God's Word?_____

_____

_____

You must renew your mind so that you begin thinking in agreement with God's Word. Many times you draw your own conclusions about God because of other people's experiences, or because of the teachings of men. These ideas that keep you from putting your complete confidence in God's Word are reasonings contrary to the truth. Don't meditate on your own ideas or someone's philosophy. Renew your mind to what the Word of God says and line up your faith with the truth. When you renew your mind to the truth of God's Word, you'll prove to yourself what His perfect will is for you. Sometimes Christians allow their faith to work against them because they believe the lies of the enemy instead of the truth. You can know that God wants you to have abundant life because of His wonderful promises. You can renew your mind to His faithfulness and know His perfect will for your life by meditating upon His Word.

You need to meditate upon His Word day and night and put it in your heart so you can really put your trust in Him. If you won't keep your mind off of your problem and begin to meditate on God's answer, you'll never completely trust Him.

Psalm 1:1-3 shows the benefits of meditating upon God's Word: ₁*Blessed (happy, fortunate, prosperous, and enviable) is the man who walks and lives not in the counsel of the ungodly...nor stands...in the path where sinners walk, nor sits down...where the scornful...gather.* ₂*But his **delight** and **desire** are in the law of the Lord, and on His law (the precepts, the instructions, the teachings of God) he **habitually** meditates (ponders and studies) by day and by night.* ₃*And He shall be like a tree firmly planted [and tended] by the streams of water, ready to bring forth its fruit in its season; its leaf also shall not fade or wither; and **everything** he does shall prosper.* (AMP)

According to verse 1, what does it mean to be blessed?_____

_____

Who will receive these blessings in their lives? (verse 2)_____

_____

_____

What is the benefit of delighting in God's Word and meditating on it day and night? What will your life be like if you'll fill your mind with His Word? (verse 3)_____

_____

_____

_____

112

According to the original Hebrew text, the word translated "meditate" means "to ponder," "to imagine," "to mutter," "to study," and "to speak."

According to this definition, what will you be doing when you're meditating on God's promises? Explain._____

_____

_____

Have you been meditating on God's Word? Think about your situation. Have you been thinking about your concerns and filling your heart with worry and doubt, or have you been meditating on God's promises and filling your heart with faith? Explain._____

_____

_____

Look at verse 2 again. What is a habit? What does it mean to habitually meditate on God's Word?_____

_____

_____

Those who habitually meditate upon God's Word day and night are the ones who will be able to trust Him under any circumstance. They'll know His promises. They'll be confident of His faithfulness. His promise will always look bigger than the problem they face. God's Word says that those who keep their minds fixed on Him will be blessed, happy, prosperous, and envied, and will have God's perfect peace (Isaiah 26:3).

When you meditate on God's Word, you're putting it in your heart. When God's Word enters your heart, you'll be able to completely put your trust in Him — which brings you to the next step.

Step 3: "For it will be pleasant if you keep them in your mind (believing them)."

The third step in this passage says that when you keep your mind fixed on God's promises, faith will rise up in your heart. The truth of God's Word will transfer from your head to your heart as you apply your mind to the knowledge of His Word.

Read Romans 10:17. *So then faith cometh by hearing, and hearing by the word of God.* (KJV)

How does faith come? How can your faith grow?_____

_____

Faith comes by hearing and meditating on the Word of God. The more time you spend filling your heart with the promises He has given you, the stronger your faith will grow. We see in Psalm 119:97 that David meditated upon God's Word and it brought him to a point of complete confidence in God's promises: *Oh, how I love your law! I meditate on it all day long.* (NIV) As David meditated on God's Word, he began to rejoice in it. David said in Psalm 119:111, *"Your testimonies have I taken as a heritage forever, for they are the rejoicing of my heart."* (AMP) In Psalm 119:162 he says, *"I rejoice at Your word as one who finds great spoil."* (AMP)

Have you been rejoicing in the promises God has given to you? Why or why not?

_____

_____

David rejoiced in God's Word because he fully trusted Him to fulfill what He had promised. David overcame fear and doubt because he meditated on God's Word. In Psalm 86:2 he declares his confidence: *O my God, save your servant, for I trust in You [leaning and believing on you, committing all and confidently looking to you, **without fear or doubt**].* (AMP)

How does this scripture describe David's trust in God?_____

_____

As you meditate on God's promises, fear and doubt will no longer be able to keep you from trusting His Word. As you put God's Word in your heart, you'll begin to rejoice in it. When it enters your heart, you'll be confident of what you hope for and convinced of what you can't see — which brings you to the next step.

Step 4: "Your lips will be accustomed to (confessing) them."

According to this scripture, when you believe God's promises, what will you be accustomed to doing?_____

_____

The fourth step in this passage states that once you believe God's Word, you'll be accustomed to confessing what you believe. The Bible states that this action follows believing.

"Accustomed" means to be in the habit of. According to this definition, what does it mean to be accustomed to confessing what you believe?_____

_____

Luke 6:45 says: *Of the abundance of the heart his mouth speaketh.* (KJV)

What you fill your heart with will come out of your mouth. What you truly believe is what you'll speak. In other words, if you fill your heart with God's promises of abundance, then you'll confidently speak of God's promises coming to pass in your life. You envision yourself abundantly blessed. If you fill your mind with your financial problem, you'll speak of lack. Worry and concern will come out of your mouth. Pay attention to what you've been speaking, and you'll know what you truly believe. This principle is stated once again in II Corinthians 4:13: *It is written: "I believed; therefore I have spoken." With that same spirit of faith we also believe and therefore speak.* (NIV)

What is the "spirit of faith"? What action does faith take?_____

_____

Believing in your heart + Confessing with your mouth = FAITH

When you're **completely trusting** in God's Word, whether it's for your children, your health, your marriage, your family's protection, the fulfillment of God's plan for your life, or whatever your situation may be, you'll speak in agreement with what God has promised in His Word.

For example: If you fill your heart with the promises of God concerning your children, you'll begin to speak in agreement with God's Word in this area of your life.

- I'll train my children in the ways of the Lord and when they grow up, they won't depart from it (Proverbs 22:6).

- My children will be blessed and mighty upon the earth (Psalm 112:2).

- My children will be disciples of the Lord, taught by Him and obedient to His will, and their peace will be great (Isaiah 54:13).

- I'll correct my children, and they'll give me rest. They'll be a delight to my heart (Proverbs 29:17).

You'll speak the Word of God because it's what you believe in your heart. Your lips will be accustomed to speaking God's promises because you're confident that His Word is true. You have a confident expectation that God will perform what He has promised. You're saying "Amen, so be it in my life!" to the promises of God!

Explain, according to Proverbs 22:17-19, the four steps that will bring you to a place of complete trust in God.

1. _____

2. _____

3. _____

4. _____

What does the Bible say the result will be if you follow these four steps? (Proverbs 22:19)

_____

_____

Use this process for whatever situation you face. Find a promise in God's Word and fix your mind on it. It will become more real to you than the problem you face, and you'll be able to truly put your trust in God. When you fill your mind with God's Word, there's no room for doubt and fear to dominate your thinking. Instead, you'll have perfect peace about your situation as you trust in what God has promised.

Read Isaiah 26:3-4. *You will guard him and keep him in perfect and constant peace **whose mind...is stayed on You** because he commits himself to You, leans on You, and hopes confidently in You.* (AMP)

Who will God keep in perfect and constant peace?_____

_____

Your spirit is much like your body. If you don't feed your body, you'll lose strength and begin to starve. If you don't feed your spirit by meditating on God's Word, you'll lose strength and begin to weaken in the midst of a trial. You have to feed your spirit every day, just as you feed your body, or you won't have His strength or be able to trust Him in every situation. If you want to walk in abundant life, you must feed on God's Word (Matthew 4:4).

SUMMARY

Fear and doubt will keep you from putting your complete trust in God. You can overcome these obstacles by seeking His Word and meditating on His promises. When you meditate on God's Word, you're putting it in your heart. As you fill your heart with His promises, your faith will grow strong and you'll be able to trust Him in every situation.

PERSONAL APPLICATION

Recall the need or desire you wrote down in the Personal Application in Lesson 7. What do you want to be able to really trust God to do?

1. _____
_____

2. _____
_____

In order to grow to the point where you can really trust God with this situation, you must follow the instructions He has given you in His Word. You must apply Proverbs 22:17-19 to your situation.

1. Consent and submit to the words of God.

   What is God's will concerning this situation in your life? What has God promised you? Recall the scriptures or the promises in which you have put your hope.

   Situation #1

   a. _____
   b. _____
   c. _____
   d. _____
   e. _____

   Situation #2

   a. _____
   b. _____
   c. _____
   d. _____
   e. _____

2. Apply your mind to the knowledge God has given you.

   Memorize these scriptures and begin to meditate on God's Word. Think about what He has promised you day and night. If you'll keep your mind focused on the promises in His Word, faith will begin to rise in your heart. You'll be equipped to cast down every worry, doubt or thought that's contrary to the truth. You'll replace these thoughts with His promises!

3. It will be pleasant if you keep God's Word in your mind, believing His promises.

   As you keep your mind on God's promises, they'll enter your heart and you'll begin to rejoice in them. You'll be convinced that God is able and willing to perform them in your life. Remember, Romans 10:17 tells you that faith comes by hearing and meditating on God's Word.

4. Your lips will be accustomed to confessing the promises of God.

   You'll know when God's Word has truly entered into your heart by whether or not you speak in agreement with His promises. You'll be accustomed to confessing His Word over your situation. When God's Word is in your heart, you'll boldly declare His promises to be true in your life!

You have control over what you choose to think about. If you choose to continue to think about your worries and concerns, you'll fill your heart with doubt and you'll fail to receive what God has promised. If you choose to fill your mind with His Word, your faith will grow and you'll receive the wonderful plan He has for your life.

REVIEW QUESTIONS

1. What two things will keep you from putting your complete confidence in God's Word?
   _____

2. How can you overcome fear and doubt? What four steps will bring you to the place of trust?_____
   _____
   _____
   _____

3. What should you do when thoughts of worry and concern come into your mind? With what should you replace these thoughts?_____
   _____
   _____

4. How can you have a life that is blessed, happy, prosperous, and successful? (Psalm 1:1-3)
   _____
   _____

5. Upon which scriptures have you been meditating? If you haven't been filling your mind with God's Word, which scriptures are you going to begin to put into your heart?
   _____
   _____

PRAYER

Lord, I want to build a stronger relationship with You. I will diligently seek You. I want to live a life that is pleasing in Your sight. I know that as I meditate on Your Word and put Your words in my heart, I will know You more intimately and learn to trust You more. I will habitually meditate on Your promises because I know You're faithful and will fulfill them in my life as I put my trust in You. In Jesus' name I pray. Amen.

Lesson 11
Recognizing and Overcoming Hindrances to Receiving God's Promises

PURPOSE

To examine three hindrances that keep many of God's people from inheriting all that He has promised them. You'll learn how you can be an overcomer and receive God's wonderful plan for your life.

OVERVIEW

You now know that to be able to walk in abundant life and receive what God has promised, you must put your absolute trust in His Word. In this lesson you'll examine three main reasons Christians fail to inherit God's promises:

1. They lack knowledge of His Word.
2. They exalt their circumstances above His promises.
3. They lack patience.

It's vital that you learn to recognize these obstacles if you want to live the abundant life God has for you. In this lesson, you'll learn how to overcome these hindrances and stand strong on God's Word. When you make a decision to do this, you'll receive all He has promised for your life.

DISCUSSION

I. Three reasons many Christians fail to inherit God's promises:

1. The first reason many of God's people fail to receive what He has promised is because they don't know His will for them.

Read Hosea 4:6. *My people are destroyed for lack of knowledge.* (KJV)

God says that it's a "lack of knowledge" that destroys His people. Because of this lack of knowledge, Christian marriages are destroyed and relationships with children are broken. Sickness, poverty, and hopelessness destroy many Christian's lives simply because they don't know God's Word.

Many of God's people don't know He has promised them victory in every situation. They don't know of the wonderful promises that belong to them through Christ Jesus. They don't understand that their Heavenly Father truly loves them and has a wonderful plan for their lives. They don't know; so, they can't receive. If the devil can keep you from the true knowledge of God, he can destroy your life. John 10:10 says that the thief comes to destroy, but Jesus came so you can have abundant life.

In II Peter 1:3-4, the Bible teaches that God has given you everything you need to live an abundant life **through your knowledge of Jesus**. Through Christ Jesus, God has given you great and precious promises so that you can live a victorious life.

Read Proverbs 11:9. *Through knowledge shall the just be delivered.* (KJV)

According to this scripture, how can you be delivered out of every trial you face?

_____

Read Proverbs 24:3-4. *₃Through skillful and godly Wisdom is a house (a life, a home, a family) built, and by understanding it is established [on a sound and good foundation], ₄And **by knowledge** shall its chambers [of every area] be filled with all precious and pleasant riches.* (AMP)

How can you experience the abundant blessings and promises of God in every area of your life?_____

_____

_____

You mustn't lack knowledge of God's Word if you want to experience the abundant life He has for you.

2.   The second reason many of God's people don't inherit His promises is that they <u>exalt</u> their circumstances above His promises.

According to *The Random House College Dictionary*, the word "exalt" means "to elevate in rank, honor or power." Sadly enough, many Christians know God's promises, but they choose to focus on their problems, thus, in their own minds, elevating the power of their circumstances over God's Word. Often they reason God's promises away by meditating on their impossible circumstances instead of realizing that nothing is impossible with God.

We'll study the lives of God's people who exalted their situation above what God promised them, and therefore didn't receive His promise. Be careful not to follow their example.

Read Numbers 13:1-2.

What had God promised to give His people?_____

_____

Read Numbers 13:25-29.

The Israelites returned from searching the land God had promised them. They had discovered that it was a land flowing with milk and honey, a land of abundance. They saw the wonderful plan God had for them; however, there were obstacles in their way. Certain circumstances caused them to question God's promise.

What did the Israelites discover about the people who occupied the land? What obstacles did they face? (verse 28)_____

_____

_____

Just like the Israelites, you now have knowledge of God's Word and have discovered the wonderful plan that He has for your life. What are some of the great and precious promises He has given you?_____

_____

_____

_____

Perhaps, also just like the Israelites, you have obstacles standing in your way. Many times these circumstances seem impossible to overcome. What obstacles seem to be in the way of inheriting what God has promised to you? What circumstances are you facing?

_____

_____

_____

_____

_____

Read Numbers 13:30.

Caleb was a man who believed God. He didn't care how strong the people were who lived in the land of Canaan, and he didn't care how big the walls were. His faith didn't weaken when he considered the impossible situation. He didn't allow the circumstances to cause him to reason God's promise away. What did he say in this scripture? _____

_____

_____

_____

_____

Because he focused his attention on God's promise, Caleb believed they could overcome any obstacle. He added faith to God's promise. He believed it with his heart; therefore, he confessed it to be true with his mouth. He confirmed his faith in God's Word by boldly declaring God's promise to be true in his life.

Read Numbers 13:31-33.

Did the children of Israel exalt God's promise when they observed their circumstances, or did they exalt their impossible situation? Did they focus their attention on the problem or the promise? Explain._____

_____

_____

_____

Read Numbers 14:1-4.

The children of Israel complained against God as they focused on their circumstances. They were consumed with their problem and, therefore, chose to doubt His promise.

Have you been following the example of the Israelites concerning a desire or a need you have in your life? Have you been elevating your circumstances' power above the power of God's Word? Does your situation cause you to question God's promise? Explain.

_____

_____

_____

Read Numbers 14:5-9.

Joshua and Caleb trusted in God's Word. They knew their God was able to fulfill His promise and give them the land of Canaan. Their God was bigger than any circumstance they faced. They tried to convince God's people to keep their eyes on His promise. They said, "Fear not, do not let your circumstances cause you to doubt God's promise. If you will only trust in God, He will give us this land of abundance just as He promised." God's people, however, wouldn't be persuaded to trust in Him. They rebelled and focused on their circumstances, and their hearts filled with fear and doubt. Fear is the opposite of faith. Fear and doubt are enemies of God's Word. They keep you from receiving His wonderful plan for your life.

Read Numbers 14:10-11.

God speaks about His people in this scripture. What does He say about them failing to trust Him? _____

_____

_____

It grieves God's heart when you doubt His Word. He longs to be gracious to you and fulfill the desires of your heart. All He requires is that you simply trust Him. Hebrews 11:6 says that without faith it's impossible to please God. He is able to do exceeding abundantly above your highest prayers, desires, hopes and dreams if you'll only choose to believe.

Isaiah 30:18 says: *The Lord [earnestly] waits [expecting, looking and longing] to be gracious to you; and therefore He lifts Himself up, that He may have mercy on you and show loving-kindness to you. For the Lord is a God of justice. Blessed (happy, fortunate, to be envied) are all those who [earnestly] wait for Him, who* **expect** *and look and long for Him [for His victory, His favor, His love, His peace, His joy, and His matchless, unbroken companionship].* (AMP)

What does God long to do for you?_____

_____

Who is blessed by God? What is God waiting for you to do ?_____

_____

_____

This scripture reveals that God longs to be gracious to you and give you all He has promised. He's waiting for you to put your trust in Him. Those who expect and look for God to fulfill His promises in their lives are the ones who will be abundantly blessed by Him. He longed to give the children of Israel the land of Canaan; but they weren't able to receive it because they chose to doubt His promise. God longs to fulfill the desires of your heart; but if you follow the example of the Israelites, you, too, will miss out on His wonderful plan.

In Genesis 18:1-14, when God told Abraham that He would give him a son, Sarah laughed and said, "How can that be? That would be impossible as I am way past childbearing years." Many times God's promises do seem impossible and we respond just as Sarah did. We think, "How can that happen? You don't know my situation — it would be a miracle if God fulfilled the desire of my heart!" If we can't see how it could happen, we often don't believe it. But God is saying to you today the same thing He said to Sarah, **"Is anything too difficult for Me?"** He was saying that **nothing** is impossible for Him. If your situation looks impossible, rejoice! It's possible. If God promised to fulfill the desires of your heart, then He is capable of bringing it to pass. Don't ask how — simply believe!

3. The third reason many of God's people fail to inherit His promises is because they lack patience.

Read Hebrews 6:12. *That ye be not slothful, but followers of them who through faith and patience inherit the promises.* (KJV)

What do you have to add to your faith in order to receive God's promises? _____

_____

"Patience" means:
- endurance through any trial
- the quality that refuses to give up
- the quality that doesn't surrender to circumstances or give up under trial
- perseverance and persistence

Many of God's people aren't willing to endure and be patient. They're not willing to wait on God to fulfill His promises. When their circumstances don't change quickly, they become impatient and give up.

God doesn't promise anywhere in the Bible that you can put a time limit or a date on when He will answer your prayer or fulfill His promise in your life. If you could, it would eliminate the need for patience. When people give God a deadline, they often end up disappointed. You have to be willing to endure any trial and be determined to receive all that God has for you. The Bible assures you in James 1:2-4 that if you persevere, patience will do a work in you and you won't lack any good thing.

Read Hebrews 10:35-36.

In verse 35, what does God's Word tell you not to do? _____

_____

_____

What does verse 36 say that you need? Why? _____

_____

_____

Many of God's people throw away their confidence in God's Word when they don't see immediate results. You need to take on the quality that doesn't surrender to circumstances — the quality that refuses to give up. Be determined that no matter how things appear or how long you have to wait, you'll receive God's promises!

II. How can you overcome all three of these obstacles and inherit all God has promised?

1. The first thing you must do to walk in abundant life and receive the promises of God is fill your mind with the knowledge of His Word.

Proverbs 18:15 says *the mind of the prudent is ever getting knowledge, and the ear of the wise is ever seeking (inquiring for and craving) knowledge.* (AMP)

What does the wise man seek? With what does he fill his mind?_____

_____

The Bible says that the wise man fills his mind with the knowledge of God's Word. He diligently seeks the wisdom of God.

Read Proverbs 2:1-5.

What does God instruct you to do in order to discover His knowledge and wisdom?
verse 1_____

_____

verse 2_____

_____

verse 3_____

_____

verse 4_____

_____

Why is it important to find the knowledge of God? (Hosea 4:6)_____

_____

Seek the knowledge of God's Word, as if you were searching for hidden treasures, so you can overcome lack of knowledge. Don't depend on others to teach you. Be willing to take the time to study for yourself. The Holy Spirit is your teacher, and He will guide you into all truth. He will do this as you study God's Word. Don't use the excuse that you don't have time to study the Word of God. You make time for whatever is most important in your life. Acts 17:11 says that the wisest of God's people will search the Scriptures daily to make sure that what they're being taught is true. God and His Word should take first place in your life. If you don't have time to spend with God in His Word, then He isn't first in your life. If the devil can keep you from studying, then lack of knowledge will keep you from receiving the promises of God.

Read Psalm 9:10.

Who will be able to trust in God?_____

_____

Who will God not fail?_____

_____

Who will God reward? (Hebrews 11:6)_____

_____

The Bible teaches that those who **know** God will be able to put their trust in Him. You can get to know God by seeking the knowledge of His Word. If you don't spend time studying His Word and praying every day, you'll never know your Heavenly Father well enough to trust Him. The most important thing you can do in your Christian life is build a strong personal relationship with God and make Him your best friend. When you grow in the knowledge of how much your Heavenly Father loves you, and when you realize He has a wonderful plan for your life, you'll put your trust in Him and receive all He has promised.

2. The second thing you must do if you want to receive all God has planned for you is exalt His promises above your circumstances.

Second Corinthians 10:5 says *Refute arguments and theories and reasonings and every proud and lofty thing that sets itself up against the [true] knowledge of God; and we lead every thought and purpose away captive into the obedience of Christ.* (AMP)

This scripture explains that you should never allow anyone's opinions, arguments, or reasonings to be exalted above God's Word. The *King James Version* says to cast down every imagination that exalts itself above the knowledge of God.

The Word of God must be the final authority in your life. Never allow your own imaginations or reasonings to convince you that anything but God's Word is true. Never allow other people's ideas to cause you to disregard His promises. Bring every thought in line with the truth of His Word. Don't allow yourself to think thoughts that are contrary to what He has promised.

How can you protect yourself from falling into deception by reasoning contrary to the truth?

_____

Read Colossians 2:6-8.

In order to learn more about Jesus, you must study God's Word. The Bible teaches that the Word and Jesus are one and the same (John 1:1 & 14). To better understand how to apply these scriptures in your life, read these verses replacing "God's Word" for the word "Jesus."

Verse 6:   As you have therefore received God's Word, walk and regulate your life and conduct yourself in union with and conformity to the Word of God.

Verse 7a: Have the roots (of your being) firmly and deeply planted in God's Word, fixed and founded on His Word.

Verse 7b: Continually build yourself up in the Word.

Verse 7c: Becoming increasingly more confirmed and established in your faith.

(Adapted from the Amplified Bible)

How can you become more established in your faith?_____

_____

_____

As you build yourself up in God's Word by meditating on it, you'll become more confirmed and established in your faith. Romans 10:17 says that faith comes by hearing and meditating on the Word of God.

Colossians 2:8 says that if you'll build yourself up in God's Word and conform your life to it, you won't be deceived by man's philosophy and intellectualism. If you know the truth of God's Word, you won't follow the traditions of men; and when you're established in your faith, you'll exalt the truth of God's promises above every circumstance you face.

Now look at the lives of God's people who exalted His promise above their circumstances and thus they received what He had planned for them.

Read II Chronicles 20: 1-2.

What difficult situation or problem faced King Jehoshaphat?_____

_____

_____

Read II Chronicles 20: 3-4.

How did Jehoshaphat respond to His difficult circumstances?_____

_____

_____

Read II Chronicles 20:5-13.

King Jehoshaphat decided to seek God instead of becoming consumed by his problem. These verses say he began meditating on and speaking about God's faithfulness. He kept his eyes on God's ability to deliver them. He said, "Lord, we do not know what to do, but our eyes are upon you." He knew God had the answer to his problem.

Read II Chronicles 20:14-17.

After King Jehoshaphat sought the Lord concerning his need, what did God say to him? What promise did God give him in verse 17?_____

_____

_____

Read II Chronicles 20:18-20.

How did King Jehoshaphat respond to the promise God had given him?

_____

_____

_____

When King Jehoshaphat heard God's promise, he began worshipping and praising Him. Another definition of "exalt" according to *The Random House College Dictionary*, is "to praise; extol." When King Jehoshaphat began to praise God, he was exalting God's promise above his circumstances. In verse 20 he said, *"Have faith in the Lord your God and you will be upheld; have faith in his prophets and you will be successful."* (NIV)

According to verse 20, of what was King Jehoshaphat confident? Did he choose to worry about his problem, or did he put his trust in God's promise?_____

_____

_____

Jehoshaphat put his trust in the Word of God. He was confident that God would perform what He had promised. He knew God was faithful and would bring them victory. He exalted God's promise above his problem by choosing to praise Him for the answer.

Read II Chronicles 20:21.

What did King Jehoshaphat do in this scripture?_____

_____

_____

King Jehoshaphat began to worship and thank God for the victory before he actually received God's promise. He was confident of what he hoped for, and he was convinced of what he could not see. He thanked God for fulfilling His promise before he saw it happen.

Read II Chronicles 20:22-24.

What did God do when He saw that King Jehoshaphat exalted His promise above his impossible circumstances? When God heard His people giving Him praise and thanksgiving in the midst of their desperate situation, how did He respond?

_____

_____

_____

God brought His people victory **after** they began to sing and praise Him. It pleases God when you worship and thank Him for the victory while still in the midst of your trial. It proves that you've really put your trust in Him. You've made a choice to praise him despite how you may feel about your situation. God will bring you victory every time if you'll follow King Jehoshaphat's example and exalt His Word.

Read II Chronicles 20:25-30.

What was the result of King Jehoshaphat's decision to put his trust in God? How did God reward his faith?_____

_____

_____

_____

How can you apply King Jehoshaphat's example in your own life? What must you do to follow his example and receive God's promises?

verse 4 _____

verse 20 _____

verse 21 _____

If you'll follow the example of King Jehoshaphat and seek God with your whole heart, exalt His promises above your circumstances, and thank Him for the answer before it comes, you'll also receive what God has promised.

3. The third thing you must do to inherit the promises of God is practice patience.

Develop the quality that doesn't surrender to circumstances — the quality that refuses to give up under trial. There's always a waiting period between the time you begin to trust God and when the promise is fulfilled. That's why God said, "through faith and *patience* you will inherit the promises."

Read James 1:2-4.

According to verse 2, how should you respond when you encounter trials and your faith is tested? _____

_____

What does proving your faith bring out in you? (verse 3) _____

_____

What will happen if you let patience (endurance) have its perfect work and you don't give up? (verse 4)_____

_____

The only way you can be truly joyful when you're going through a trial is to look past your circumstances and keep your eyes on God's promise. If you're truly convinced that His Word is true, then you'll rejoice in His promise. You'll realize that your difficult circumstances are only temporary. God's Word is the truth that will become a reality in your life. God has promised to deliver you out of every problem you may face. When you're joyful while you wait, you'll see the faithfulness of God.

We've all been tempted to give up when our circumstances didn't change quickly. It's during this waiting period that many of God's people waver and give up. Jesus shows, through His own experience of temptation, how to react to the devil so you can be strengthened and remain patient when your faith is tested.

Read Matthew 4: 1-11.

According to verses 4, 7 & 10, how did Jesus respond when He was tried and tempted?

_____

_____

_____

When Jesus' faith was tried, His response was, "It is written." He spoke the Word of God, and God's Word strengthened Him in the midst of His trial. When your faith is tested you can follow Jesus' example and overcome the temptation to give up by speaking what God has promised to you. It worked for Jesus, and it will work for you. He's your example.

If you're struggling with a financial situation and facing difficult circumstances, you may be tempted to get discouraged and give up. If you'll begin to speak the Word of God, you'll strengthen your faith and overcome this temptation.

Speak what God has promised you:

- It is written: *My God shall supply all of my needs.* (Philippians 4:19)

- It is written: *Many troubles may face me, but the Lord will deliver me out of them all.* (Psalm 34:19)

- It is written: *God is able to make all grace abound toward me so that I will have all of my needs met and be able to give abundantly to every good work.* (II Corinthians 9:8)

When you speak the promises of God's Word in the midst of any problem, you'll be strengthened and, therefore, can continue to be patient until your answer comes.

SUMMARY

If you want to walk in abundant life, you must do three things: 1) Seek the knowledge of God's promises as if you were searching for hidden treasures. 2) Put your trust in the Word of God by exalting His promises above every difficult circumstance you face. By filling your mind with His Word, you can cast down every imagination that causes you to question His promises. 3) Be patient. Be determined to receive all you've inherited in Christ Jesus. Take on the quality that doesn't surrender to circumstances or give up under trial. When your faith is tested and you're tempted to become discouraged and give up, strengthen yourself by speaking the Word of God. If you'll make a decision to do these three things, you'll walk in abundant life and inherit all God has promisèd.

PERSONAL APPLICATION

Self-Examination

1. What three things can keep you from inheriting what Jesus provided for you?
   a. _____
   b. _____
   c. _____

2. How can you overcome these three obstacles and inherit the promises of God in your life?
   a. _____
   b. _____
   c. _____

3. Have you been seeking the Wisdom and knowledge found in God's Word? Are you taking time to communicate with your Heavenly Father and study His Word?

   _____

4. Have you been exalting God's Word, or your circumstances? Do you believe the power of His Word is greater than the power of your circumstances?

_____

_____

5. Have you been building yourself up in God's Word by meditating on His promises, or have you been filling your mind with your problem? Explain.

_____

_____

6. Are you following the example of the children of Israel concerning your situation, or are you following the example of King Jehoshaphat?_____

_____

7. Are you determined not to give up until the promise is fulfilled? Will you give up when your faith is tested? Have you determined in your heart that you won't surrender to circumstances or give up under trial?_____

_____

8. Which promises in God's Word will you strengthen yourself with when you're tempted to become discouraged and give up? Which scriptures will you use to combat thoughts of fear and doubt?_____

_____

Situation #1

It is written:_____

_____

It is written:_____

_____

It is written:_____

_____

Situation #2

It is written:_____

_____

It is written:_____

_____

It is written:_____

_____

Follow King Jehoshaphat's example and begin to worship and thank God for the victory before you see it happen!

Lesson 12

Abraham — a Man Who Trusted in God's Promises

PURPOSE

To study the life of Abraham so that you can follow his example. He was a man who put his absolute trust in God's Word and received all God had promised him.

OVERVIEW

Abraham overcame the three obstacles presented in the previous lesson, and walked in the abundant blessings of God. The Bible teaches that if you want to receive all God has promised, you must follow Abraham's example. Abraham didn't lack knowledge of God's promise. He exalted the promise above his impossible circumstances and waited patiently for God to fulfill it in his life; as a result, he received all God had planned for him. You'll also receive God's perfect plan for your life and partake of all He has promised if you'll choose to follow Abraham's example and put your absolute trust in God's Word.

DISCUSSION

I.   Abraham put his trust in God's promise.

Read Romans 4:18-21: *18[For Abraham, human reason for] hope being gone, hoped in faith that he should become the father of many nations, as he had been promised, So [numberless] shall your descendants be. 19He did not weaken in faith when he considered the [utter] impotence of his own body, which was as good as dead because he was about a hundred years old, or [when he considered] the barrenness of Sarah's [deadened] womb. 20No unbelief or distrust made him waver (doubtingly question) concerning the promise of God, but he grew strong and was empowered by faith as he gave praise and glory to God, 21Fully satisfied and assured that God was able and mighty to keep His word and to do what He had promised.* (AMP)

According to verse 18, what had God promised Abraham?_____

_____

God promised Abraham and Sarah a son. Why was this impossible in the natural? (verse 19)

_____

_____

Are you facing a situation that seems impossible to you in the natural? Explain.

_____

_____

God speaks through His Word. What promise has He given you concerning your situation?

_____

_____

_____

When all natural hope was gone, what did Abraham do? (verse 18) How can you follow Abraham's example?_____

_____

_____

According to verse 18, human reason said there was no hope for Abraham. The promise God had given him seemed physically impossible. Abraham's hope, however, didn't lie in the limitations of human possibilities. He reached beyond natural hope and hoped in faith. He knew that absolutely nothing was impossible for God. He was confident that God was able to perform what He had promised him.

When Abraham considered his impossible situation, how did it affect his faith? (verse 19)

_____

_____

According to verse 20, did Abraham question God's promise when he considered his present situation? Explain._____

_____

Abraham was surrounded by physical evidence that denied the truth of God's promise. His circumstances said, "You're too old and Sarah's barren." But what decision did Abraham make? Did he decide to exalt his circumstances, or did he choose to exalt the power of God's promise?_____

_____

Abraham exalted God's promise above his circumstances. Abraham made a quality decision about what to believe. He decided not to allow the physical evidence to cause him to doubt God's promise. He chose to believe God's Word no matter what it looked like in the natural.

What are your circumstances saying to you?_____

_____

_____

When you consider your circumstances, how does it affect your faith? Do you allow your faith to weaken when you consider the obstacles in your way? Why?_____

_____

What must you do to follow Abraham's example concerning this situation in your life? (verses 19-20) _____

_____

_____

According to verse 20, how did Abraham grow strong in faith? How can you grow strong in faith?_____

Abraham lived a life of praise and thanksgiving to God. Romans 4:20 says that Abraham's faith grew, and he was **empowered with faith as** he gave praise and glory to God. As you follow Abraham's example, your faith will grow. When you live a life of continual thanksgiving to God for all He has promised, you'll be empowered with the same faith that Abraham had. Begin today to build your faith by offering praise and thanksgiving for the many promises that are yours through Christ Jesus:

- Heavenly Father, I thank you that You're at work in my husband's heart, creating in him the desire and ability to love me like Christ loves the Church, (Philippians 2:13; Ephesians 5:25)

- Lord, I thank you that my wife is a gift from You. Your grace is at work in her creating the desire and ability to become the virtuous woman You created her to be. (Philippians 2:13; Proverbs 31:10-31)

- Heavenly Father, I thank You for Your promise concerning my children. You have said that they will be your disciples, taught by You and obedient to Your will, and their peace and undisturbed composure shall be great. (Isaiah 54:13)

- Lord, I thank You for my family's salvation. You're at work in them, putting the desire in their hearts to serve You. You've promised to draw them to Yourself; You'll deliver them from the dominion of darkness and transfer them into the kingdom of Your Son. (Acts 16:31, John 6:44, Job 22:30, Col. 1:13)

- Heavenly Father, I thank you for your promise of protection. You're my Refuge and my Fortress, and I put my trust in You. You've commanded Your angels to take charge over me, to protect me in all my ways. (Psalm 91)

- Lord, I thank You that by the stripes of Jesus I am healed. Your Word brings health and healing to all my flesh. (Isaiah 53:5, Proverbs 4:20-22)

- Heavenly Father, I thank You for Your grace that abounds toward me so that I have everything I need. I'm able to be a blessing to others and give abundantly to every good work. (II Corinthians 9:8)

- Heavenly Father, I thank You that because of Your grace, which is at work in my life, You're able to do exceeding abundantly above all that I dare ask or think — infinitely beyond my highest prayers, desires, thoughts, hopes or dreams. (Ephesians 3:20)

- Thank You Father for Your Son Jesus Who came so I can have abundant life — spiritually, physically, emotionally, socially and financially. It's only because of Jesus that I'm able to receive Your great and precious promises in my life. (John 10:10, II Corinthians 1:20)

After reading these prayers of thanksgiving, do you have a clearer understanding of how offering praise and thanksgiving to God strengthens your faith? Explain._____

_____

_____

As you remind yourself of all God's promises, you'll be encouraged and your faith will be strengthened. Romans 10:17 says that faith comes by hearing, and hearing by the Word of God. When you hear yourself thanking God for His promises, faith will rise up in your heart.

Explain Abraham's confidence in God. (verse 21) _____

_____

_____

_____

Do you have this same confidence in God? Why? _____

_____

_____

When Abraham's situation looked impossible, he put his trust in God's Word. His faith didn't weaken when he considered his circumstances. He had no unbelief or distrust, and he didn't waver concerning God's promise. He grew strong and was empowered with faith as he gave praise and thanksgiving to God. Abraham was confident not only that God was able, but also that He would do what he had promised.

Read Hebrews 6:11-15: *11But we do [strongly and earnestly] desire for each of you to show the same diligence and sincerity [all the way through] in realizing and enjoying the full assurance and development of [your] hope until the end. 12In order that you may not grow disinterested and become [spiritual] sluggards, but imitators, behaving as do those who through faith...and by practice of patient endurance and waiting are [now] inheriting the promises. 13For when God made [His] promise to Abraham, He swore by Himself, since He had no one greater by whom to swear, 14Saying, Blessing I certainly will bless you and multiplying I will multiply you. 15And so it was that he [Abraham], having waited long and endured patiently, realized and obtained...what God had promised him.* (AMP)

What two characteristics are found in those who will inherit the promises of God? (verse 12)

_____

_____

Verse 12 says that you must be diligent so that you don't become slothful and disinterested in God's Word. Many of God's people are slothful. They don't want to exert the effort to diligently seek Him; therefore, they'll never walk in the fullness of life that He has prepared for them. God is a rewarder of those who diligently seek Him (Hebrews 11:6). Those who follow Abraham's example by putting their absolute trust in God's Word, and enduring through every trial, will receive all that He has promised.

If you want to inherit the promises of God you must:

- add faith to God's promises
- add patience to your faith

Read II Corinthians 4:13. *"It is written: "I believed; therefore I have spoken." With that same spirit of faith we also believe and therefore speak.* (NIV)

What is the spirit of faith? What does it mean to add faith to God's promises?

_____

_____

_____

Believing God's promises with your heart +
confessing them to be true with your mouth = FAITH

Patience is the quality that refuses to give up. It's the quality that doesn't surrender to circumstance or give up under trial. It's characterized by a determination to receive what God has promised.

According to Hebrews 6:14, what promise did God make to Abraham?_____

_____

What quality did Abraham add to his faith before he received God's promise? How can you follow his example? (verse 15)_____

_____

Describe what it means to add patience to your faith._____

_____

_____

Abraham had the quality that doesn't surrender to circumstances or give up under trial. He waited patiently for God to fulfill His promise in his life. You must follow Abraham's example if you want to receive all God has planned for you.

II. Abraham obeyed God.

Read James 2:21-22: _21Don't you remember that even our father Abraham was declared good because of what he did, **when he was willing to obey God**, even if it meant offering his son Isaac to die on the alter? 22You see, he was **trusting God so much** that he was **willing to do whatever God told him to**; his faith was made complete by what he did, by his actions, his good deeds._ (TLB)

According to verse 22, how do you know that Abraham was completely trusting God? How was Abraham's faith made complete?_____

_____

Abraham trusted God so much that he was willing to obey Him no matter what He asked him to do. God had given Abraham a son, Isaac, as He had promised. God told Abraham that through Isaac He would give him many descendants. Then He tested Abraham's faith by asking him to sacrifice his only son. Hebrews 11:17-19 reveals that Abraham was able to obey because He trusted in what God had promised. He reasoned that God was able to raise Isaac from the dead. Abraham obeyed God because he looked to His promise. God expects you to be obedient to His Word, too. He has given you many instructions in His Word. He tells you to:

- love others (John 15:17)
- give to those in need (I John 3:17-18)
- forgive (Ephesians 4:32)
- seek Him first (Matthew 6:33)

- love your enemies (Matthew 5:44)
- do good to those who wrong you (Matthew 5:44)

When you're willing to obey God and His Word, you prove that you're really trusting Him. Your actions make your faith complete. When you're a doer of God's Word, you pass His test. He sees that you've really put your trust in Him, just as Abraham did. Proverbs 28:20 says that the faithful man will abound in blessings. You've already learned that those blessings include favor, peace, happiness, health, prosperity, prosperous relationships, and success. Deuteronomy 28:1-13 reveals that God will bless every area of your life if you'll choose to obey Him. If you'll follow Abraham's example and keep your eyes on God's promises, you'll also walk in obedience to His Word.

Are you following Abraham's example? Are you trusting God so much that you're willing to do whatever He instructs you to do? _____

III. Abraham was God's friend.

Read James 2:23. *And the scripture was fulfilled that says, "Abraham believed God, and it was credited to him as righteousness," and he was called God's friend.* (NIV)

Why was Abraham called God's friend? _____

_____

Notice that it wasn't because Abraham **believed in** *God* that he was called His friend. It was because Abraham **believed God**. Abraham believed that God would fulfill whatever He had promised. Many people believe in God, but very few believe, like Abraham, that God will perform what He has promised.

How can you be God's friend? _____

_____

SUMMARY

When Abraham considered his impossible circumstances, he put his hope in God's promise. He knew that what seemed impossible in the natural wasn't impossible with God. As he lived a life of thanksgiving, he grew strong and was empowered by faith. Abraham trusted God so much that he was willing to do whatever he was told. He received all of God's promises because he chose to put his trust in God. Abraham's marriage was blessed; his children were blessed; he was prosperous and successful; he lived a long healthy life; his prayers were answered, and he obtained the desires of his heart. Most important, he was God's friend because he chose to believe Him. Abraham's life, therefore, was full of God's blessings, and he received God's plan for his life. You can live a life that is full of God's blessings, and you can receive His perfect plan for you if you'll follow Abraham's example and add faith and patience to His promises. God loves you as much as He loved Abraham. God is not a respecter of persons; however, He is a rewarder of those who trust and obey Him. You can expect to receive God's promises if you'll follow Abraham's example and choose to put your trust in His Word.

PERSONAL APPLICATION

The Bible teaches that in order to inherit God's promises, you must follow Abraham's example. Examine yourself to see if your life resembles the life of Abraham.

SELF-EXAMINATION

Situation #1

What difficult circumstances are you facing?_____
_____
_____

Write the promises that you're standing on. What has God promised you?

a. _____
_____

b. _____
_____

c. _____
_____

d. _____
_____

e. _____
_____

Personalize Romans 4:18-21.

_____'s human reason for hope being gone, hoped in faith that _____
    (insert your name)

_____
_____
_____
_____

                    (write what God has promised you)
as he/she had been promised,_____didn't weaken in faith when he/she considered
                    (insert your name)

_____
_____
_____
_____

               (write the circumstances that you are facing)
No unbelief or distrust made_____waver concerning the promise of God, but
                (insert your name)

_____ grew strong in faith as he/she gave praise and glory to God, fully satisfied
    (insert your name)
and assured that God was able and mighty to keep His Word and to do what He had promised.

Read the passage several times. Ask yourself, "Do I have the same assurance that Abraham had? Am I fully satisfied and assured that God is able and mighty to keep His Word and to do what He has promised?"

Write a prayer of thanksgiving concerning this situation. Begin to thank God for the promises He has given you.

_____
_____
_____
_____
_____

Situation #2

What difficult circumstances are you facing?_____
_____
_____

Write the promises that you're standing on. What has God promised you?

a._____
_____

b._____
_____

c._____
_____

d._____
_____

e._____
_____

Personalize Romans 4:18-21.

_____'s human reason for hope being gone, hoped in faith that _____
(insert your name)
_____
_____
_____

(write what God has promised you)
as he/she had been promised,_____didn't weaken in faith when he/she considered
(insert your name)
_____
_____
_____

(write the circumstances that you are facing)
No unbelief or distrust made _____waver concerning the promise of God, but
(insert your name)
_____ grew strong in faith as he/she gave praise and glory to God, fully satisfied
(insert your name)
and assured that God was able and mighty to keep His Word and to do what He had promised.

Read the passage several times. Ask yourself, "Do I have the same assurance that Abraham had? Am I fully satisfied and assured that God is able and mighty to keep His Word and to do what He has promised?"

Write a prayer of thanksgiving concerning this situation. Begin to thank God for the promises He has given you.

_____
_____
_____
_____

Are you following Abraham's example?
Have you put your trust in God?

Lesson 13
The Children of Israel — God's People Who Didn't Trust in His Promises

PURPOSE

To study the lives of the children of Israel so you can make sure you aren't following their example. They were God's people, but they didn't put their trust in Him; therefore, they didn't inherit His promises for their lives.

OVERVIEW

You've studied the life of Abraham and realized that you must follow his example if you want to receive all that God has promised. In this lesson, you'll look at the lives of God's people who didn't trust in His Word. They were descendants of Abraham, and heirs to all the blessings that God had given him. But unlike Abraham, they allowed their circumstances to cause them to doubt God's promises. Worry and fear caused them to miss out on the plan God had for their lives. They rebelled against God by refusing to believe Him and choosing to disobey His Word. The Bible tells us that the story of the Israelites was written to warn against following their example. It was written so that you can be aware of the consequences of not putting your trust in God. As you study the lives of the children of Israel, examine your own life to make sure you aren't making the same mistakes that will keep you from receiving all God has promised.

DISCUSSION

In Lesson 11 you learned that God promised the children of Israel the land of Canaan. It was a land of abundance, a land flowing with milk and honey. God promised the Israelites abundant blessings if they would put their trust in Him. But when their faith was tested, they chose to worry and complain instead. God loved His people, and He was patient with them because He longed to give them what He had promised. But they rebelled against Him by refusing to trust and obey His Word. As a result, they didn't receive the wonderful plan that God had prepared and provided for them. They failed to receive His promise.

God has prepared and provided a life of abundance for you, just as He did for the Israelites. His will for His children hasn't changed (and doesn't). He has promised you a life full of joy, peace, love, victory, success, health and prosperity — a life in which He is able to do exceedingly above your highest prayers, desires, hopes and dreams. Your Heavenly Father loves you and longs to fill your life with His blessings. All that He asks is that you simply trust and obey His Word. If you choose to go the way of the children of Israel, however, you too will miss out on God's perfect plan. Study the lives of the children of Israel so you can learn from their mistakes and avoid following in their footsteps.

Read Hebrews 3:7-19. *7Therefore, as the Holy Spirit says: Today, if you will hear His voice, 8Do not harden your hearts, as [happened] in the rebellion [of Israel] and their provocation and embitterment [of Me] in the day of testing in the wilderness, 9Where your fathers tried [My patience] and tested [My forbearance] and found I stood their test, and they saw My works for forty years. 10And so I was provoked (displeased and sorely grieved) with that generation, and said, They always err and are led astray in their hearts, and they have not perceived or recognized My ways and become progressively better and more experimentally and intimately acquainted with them. 11Accordingly, I swore in My wrath and indignation, They shall not enter My rest. 12[Therefore* **beware**] **brethren**, *take care, lest there be in any one of you a* **wicked, unbelieving heart** *[which refuses to cleave to, trust in, and rely on Him], leading you to turn away and desert or stand aloof from the living God. 13But* **instead warn** *(admonish, urge, and encourage) one another every day, as long as it is called Today, that none of you may be hardened [into settled rebellion] by the deceitfulness of sin....14For we have become fellows with Christ (the Messiah) and share in all He has for us,* **if only** *we hold our first newborn confidence and original assured expectation...firm and unshaken to the end. 15Then while it is [still] called Today, if you would hear His voice and when you hear it, do not harden your hearts as in the rebellion [in the desert, when the people provoked and irritated and embittered God against them]. 16For who were they who heard and yet were rebellious and provoked [Him]? Was it not all those who came out of Egypt led by Moses? 17And with whom was He irritated and provoked and grieved for forty years? Was it not with those who sinned, whose dismembered bodies were strewn and left in the desert? 18And to whom did He swear that they should not enter His rest, but to those who disobeyed [who had not listened to His word and who refused to be compliant or be persuaded]? 19So we see that they were not able to enter [into His rest], because of their unwillingness to adhere to and trust in and rely on God [unbelief had shut them out].* (AMP)

This whole passage of scripture is about the journey of the children of Israel from bondage and slavery into the land God had promised them. This generation never reached the promised land because they chose to focus on their circumstances rather than to put their trust in God. First Corinthians 10:1-11 says that the story of the children of Israel was written to warn you not to follow their example.

Just like the Israelites, many times you find yourself in a difficult situation (sickness, lack, confusion, difficult marriage relationship, problems with children, or circumstances that you want to change). God wants to take you out of those difficult situations and bring you into what He has promised. But He wants you to completely trust Him in this process. You must recognize attitudes and actions in your own life that resemble those of the children of Israel so that you don't fail to receive what God has promised. As you study this passage of scripture, think about one area of your life in which you want to see change — an area in which you want to receive victory and enter into God's best for your life.

In what situation would you like to see change take place? What do you need or want God to do?_____

_____

_____

_____

What circumstances seem to keep you from the desire of your heart? What obstacles are in your way?_____

_____

_____

What has God promised in His Word concerning this situation? In which promises of God have you placed your hope?

1. _____

_____

2. _____

_____

3. _____

_____

4. _____

_____

5. _____

_____

Read Hebrews 3:7-8.

According to these verses, what is the Holy Spirit saying to you ?_____

_____

In verse 8 the Holy Spirit warns you not to harden your heart to God's Word when your faith is being tested. Many times, when you begin to put your trust in a promise from God, your circumstances don't change immediately because the enemy comes against you with circumstances designed to try your faith. The Holy Spirit warns you not to become angry and give up during this time of testing; otherwise, you'll live a defeated life. Don't follow the example of the Israelites. When your faith is tested, you mustn't harden your heart to God's Word.

What does it mean to harden your heart? Hebrews 3:18–19 shows two ways in which the children of Israel hardened their hearts toward God.

1. The first way the Israelites hardened their hearts was through unbelief.

God told them He would bring them into the promised land, but they exalted their circumstances above the power of God's Word. Because it seemed impossible for God's promise to really come to pass, they reasoned His promise away and hardened their hearts through unbelief.

Look at a promise God has given you. See if you've been following their example: In Psalm 37:4 God has given you a promise concerning the desires of your heart, *Delight yourself in the Lord and He will give you the desires and secret petitions of your heart.* (AMP) If you reason this promise away because of circumstances in your life, your unbelief is hardening your heart to His Word. When you disregard God's promise for any *reason* it causes your heart to become hardened. If you hear a promise that He has given in His Word and you choose not to put your trust in it because it seems impossible, then you've chosen to follow the example of the children of Israel.

Have you hardened your heart to this promise from God, or have you chosen to trust God to bring to pass the desires of your heart? Explain._____

_____

2. The second way the Israelites hardened their heart was through disobedience.

The children of Israel refused to change their ways. They became angry and discouraged in their circumstances, and were deceived into believing that obedience to God wasn't profitable. Through disobedience, they hardened their hearts to God's Word

Have you been hardening your heart toward God by disobeying Him in an area of your life? (In your finances, your marriage, your children, etc.).

Read Hebrews 3:8.

What did the Israelites do when they were faced with a trial? How did they handle the testing of their faith?_____

_____

The children of Israel rebelled when they were faced with trials. They refused to believe God's Word or obey His instructions. Many times your circumstances don't change immediately when you begin to put your trust in God. Often there's a time of testing and enduring, a time of choosing to believe God's Word in the midst of your circumstances. When your faith is tested and your prayers don't seem to be working, you mustn't give up and question God's Word. You mustn't disregard His promise and worry instead of trusting. If you do this, you're rebelling against God and following the example of the Israelites.

Read Hebrews 3:9.

According to this verse, the Israelites had seen God's miracles again and again for forty years. He had protected and provided for them. Still, when the circumstances became difficult and their faith was tested, they complained and worried instead of trusting God.

How do you respond when trials come your way or when circumstances look impossible?

_____

_____

Many times God's people give up and become discouraged, choosing to surrender to their circumstances. But if you'll stand strong when your faith is tested, you'll come through every trial victoriously.

Read Hebrews 3:10.

What did God say about this generation? How does God feel when you refuse to trust and obey His Word?_____

_____

_____

_____

God's heart was grieved with that generation. He said they had been led astray in their hearts because they had chosen not to believe His Word.

God is displeased, and His heart grieves when you worry instead of trusting Him. When you focus your attention on your problem instead of His promise, it grieves His heart. God longs to show Himself strong in your life. He is only waiting for you to put your trust in Him. James 1:6-7 says that if you choose to doubt God's Word, you won't receive from Him. Matthew 21:22, on the other hand, reveals that if you'll put your trust in God, you'll receive whatever you ask. God is faithful to His Word. He's not a respecter of persons. He's only looking for someone who will choose to believe Him. II Chronicles 16:9 says, *For the eyes of the Lord run to and fro throughout the whole earth, to show himself strong on behalf of them whose heart is perfect toward Him.* (KJV)

Were the hearts of the children of Israel perfect before God? Why? Did they receive God's promise?_____

_____

_____

Was Abraham's heart perfect before God? Why? Did he receive God's promise?

_____

_____

You can either have a heart hardened toward God through unbelief and disobedience, or you can have a perfect heart, by putting your trust in Him and obeying His Word.

Read Hebrews 3:11._____

_____

What were the consequences of the Israelites' sin?_____

_____

What does it mean to enter God's rest?

A dictionary will give you a clearer understanding of what it means to rest.

"Rest" means:
- freedom from anything that tires, troubles, or disturbs you
- to be free from worry and anxiety
- to have peace
- to rely, trust, or depend on someone

According to these definitions, when you enter God's rest, you have His perfect peace concerning your situation. You put your absolute trust in His Word, and rely and depend on Him. Therefore, you're free from anything that tires, troubles, or disturbs you. You're free from worry, anxiety, and fear because your confidence is in God. When you enter into His rest, God will move strongly on your behalf and accomplish His perfect plan for you. But, if you allow worry, doubt, and fear to remain in your heart, you'll fail to receive all that He has promised.

God has prepared a place of rest for His people. It's a place in your Christian life where you have perfect peace because you're satisfied and assured that God is able and willing to perform what He has promised. You aren't worried or concerned; you simply believe His Word and rest in His promise. The Israelites couldn't enter this place of rest because they rebelled against God by refusing to put their absolute trust in His promise.

Read Hebrews 3:12.

The Holy Spirit is talking to you in this scripture. He warns you against following the example of the Israelites. What does this scripture tell you to beware? _____

_____

_____

_____

Have you chosen to worry or to become discouraged about your situation instead of putting your trust in God? According to verse 12, when you do this, how does the Holy Spirit describe your heart?_____

_____

Referring again to verse 12, what does a wicked, unbelieving heart refuse to do?

_____

_____

According to this verse, when you choose not to trust in and rely on God, what does this lead you to do?_____

_____

The Holy Spirit is talking to God's people in this verse. He says that those who don't trust in God have a wicked heart. He's telling you, "Beware, brethren, lest there be found in you a wicked, unbelieving heart which refuses to trust in God!" This warning is strong because this scripture says that when you choose to worry and focus on your circumstances instead of trusting God, you're turning away and standing aloof from the living God.

According the dictionary, "aloof" means:

- to withdraw oneself
- to set apart from
- to stand at a distance

According to this, then, when you choose to become worried, discouraged, or frustrated concerning your situation, what are you actually doing toward God?_____

_____

_____

When you choose to be worried or concerned about a particular situation in your life, you're setting yourself apart from God. When you worry or become discouraged, you withdraw yourself from God's ability to help you. You stand at a distance from God when you focus your attention on your problem instead of His promise. That's why this scripture warns you not to follow the example of the children of Israel. God will never leave you; however, you can set yourself apart from Him. It's a dangerous thing to withdraw from God, not allowing Him to help you because you refuse to trust in His Word.

Read James 1:6-7. *But when he asks, he must believe and not doubt, because he who doubts is like a wave of the sea, blown and tossed by the wind. *That man should not think he will receive anything from the Lord.* (NIV)

According to this scripture, why does the Holy Spirit warn against doubting God's Word?

_____

_____

Have you set yourself apart from God by choosing to worry about your situation? Did you realize that this is what you were doing when you doubt His Word?_____

_____

Read Hebrews 3:13.

What does this verse tell you to do?_____

_____

_____

This scripture tells you that if you see people who are tempted to worry or be concerned about situations in their lives, instead of choosing to put their trust in God, you should encourage them and warn them not to harden their hearts to His Word. Every time a person hears God's Word and chooses not to act on it, he's hardening his heart. If a person refuses to act upon God's wisdom concerning their situation (marriage, children, finances, etc.), they're rebelling against God. God won't move in the life of someone who is rebelling against Him by refusing to put their complete trust in His Word.

The Holy Spirit says to warn them so that they don't fall into rebellion through the deceitfulness of sin. Many times we think of sin as stealing, killing, lying, etc. But sin can be something as simple as slothfulness, worry, doubt or unforgiveness. Anything that doesn't please God is sin. Hebrews 11:6 says that without faith it's impossible to please God. When you choose not to put your trust in God, you're rebelling against Him.

Read Hebrews 3:14.

This verse gives us the good news with which we should encourage ourselves and others. We have become fellow heirs with Christ and share in all He has provided for us.

What have you inherited in Christ Jesus? Read II Corinthians 1:20 and Galatians 3:29.

_____

According to Hebrews 3:14, what is the condition for sharing in all the promises of God?

_____

_____

If you'll hold fast to your confident expectation in God's Word, you'll share in all His promises. Are you confident that you have eternal life? Would anybody be able to convince you that you haven't received this promise? You must have this same assurance with every promise God has given in His Word. If He has given you a promise, you should have a firm belief in His honesty, truthfulness and power to fulfill that promise in your life.

Read Hebrews 3:15.

This verse also warns you against hardening your heart and rebelling against God's Word. That's what kept the children of Israel from receiving His promises. Beware following their example. Worry, doubt, unforgiveness, fear, and resentment are characteristics found in those who are rebelling against God. When you allow any of these characteristics to be present in your life, you're disobeying His Word. The children of Israel rebelled against God through unbelief and disobedience. When you choose to focus on your problem instead of God's promise, you are rebelling against Him through unbelief.

Have you rebelled against God by allowing some of these characteristics to be present in your life? Have you chosen to worry instead of trusting Him? Have you chosen to hold resentment in your heart toward someone instead of forgiving them?

Read I John 1:9 and Hebrews 8:12.

If you've been rebelling against God, what encouragement can you find in these scriptures?

_____

_____

Read Hebrews 3:16-19.

What happened to the Israelites? Did they receive God's promise?_____

_____

_____

Give two reasons why the Israelites weren't able to enter into God's rest. (verses 18 & 19) What shut them out from receiving God's promises?

1. _____

2. _____

What actions and attitudes of the children of Israel should you beware of in your own life?

verse 8:_____

verse 12:_____

verse 13:_____

verse 18:_____

verse 19:_____

These scriptures show five examples of the attitudes and actions of the children of Israel. Decide not to follow their example. Examine yourself as you study each action that caused God's people to miss out on His promises.

1. They rebelled when their faith was tested. They became discouraged and gave up. They complained and murmured when faced with a trial.

2. They had wicked, unbelieving hearts. They set themselves apart from God because they chose to exalt their circumstances above the power of His promise.

3. They were hardened into rebellion through the deceitfulness of sin (worry, fear, doubt, unforgiveness, complaining, etc.).

4. They disobeyed God. They wouldn't listen to His Word. They refused to be corrected and they wouldn't change their ways. They wouldn't be compliant or persuaded to follow His wisdom.

5. They were unwilling to adhere to, trust in or rely on God. Unbelief kept them from receiving His promise.

SUMMARY

In Lesson 12 you observed the life of Abraham. He put his trust in God and received all that had been promised to him. You learned that if you'll follow his example, you, also, will receive what God has planned for you. The only way you can fail to receive God's promises is if you follow the example of the children of Israel and refuse to believe His Word. Beware any actions or attitudes in your own life that resemble those of God's people who lived defeated lives. You must imitate those who through trusting in God's Word, and enduring their trials, possessed all of God's promises. The choice is yours: you can follow either the example of Abraham or the children of Israel. There is no in-between. You'll walk in either faith or unbelief. You'll trust and obey God's Word and walk in victory, or you'll disobey and doubt His Word and walk in defeat. God has left the decision up to you. Choose abundant life and put your trust in Him!

PERSONAL APPLICATION

Read Deuteronomy 30:15-19. *15See, I have set before you life and prosperity, death and destruction. 16For I command you today to love the Lord your God, to walk in His ways, and to keep his commands, decrees and laws; then you will live and increase, and the Lord your God will bless you.. 17But if your heart turns away and you are not obedient...18I declare to you this day that you will certainly be destroyed...19This day I call heaven and earth as witnesses against you that I have set before you life and death, blessings and curses. **Now choose life**, so that you and your children may live.* (NIV)

What two choices has God set before you?

1. _____

_____

2. _____

_____

What will be the result if you choose to trust and obey God?_____

_____

What will be the result if you choose to worry and disobey?_____

_____

It's very important to make sure your life isn't reflecting the attitudes and actions of the children of Israel. Each one of God's people is following either the example of Abraham, or the example of the Israelites. This determines who receives God's promises and who walks in discouragement, defeat, and disappointment. If you want God's perfect will to come to pass in your life, decide to seek God and put your trust in His Word.

SELF-EXAMINATION

You've learned that God has given you many promises for your life on earth. Some of those promises include:

- a wonderful marriage
- children who serve and obey God
- salvation of your family
- protection
- victory over sin
- healing
- financial abundance
- success
- the fulfillment of your heart's desire
- answered prayer
- deliverance from every problem
- spiritual blessings

Hebrews 6:12 describes two different ways Christians respond to the promises of God: *That ye be not slothful, but followers of them who through faith and patience inherit the promises.*

1. Some Christians are slothful. (The children of Israel)

If you follow the example of the children of Israel, the following characteristics be present in your life:

- You doubt God's promises and disobey His Word.
- You neglect your relationship with God.
- You exalt your circumstances above the power of God's promise.
- You become discouraged when your circumstances don't change quickly. You give up when your faith is tested.

2. Some Christians add faith and patience to God's promises. (Abraham)

If you follow the example of Abraham, the following characteristics will be present in your life:

- You trust in God's promises and obey His Word.
- You diligently seek God.
- You exalt the power of God's promise above your problem.
- You don't surrender to your circumstances. You remain joyful when your faith is tested.

- You settle for your present situation even though it's not God's best.

- You set yourself apart from God by focusing on your problem instead of His promise.

- You set your mind on your problem and fill your heart with doubt.

- You're filled with worry and fear.

- You speak about your problem.

- You complain about your situation.

- You live a life of disappointment and discouragement.

- You persevere and are determined to receive God's best in every area of your life.

- You walk closely with God because you trust in His promises regardless of the problem you face.

- You set your mind on God's promises and fill your heart with faith.

- You have God's perfect peace.

- You confess God's promises to be true in your life.

- You live a life of thanksgiving to God for all He has promised you.

- You're a living testimony that God is faithful to His promises.

Recall the specific promises you've put your hope in concerning the situations in your life.

Situation #1

a. _____

b. _____

c. _____

d. _____

e. _____

Situation #2

a. _____

b. _____

c. _____

d. _____

e. _____

Look back over the characteristics found in the life of Abraham versus the children of Israel. Whose example have you been following? Explain._____

_____

_____

In the past, which characteristics of the children of Israel have been present in your life?

_____

_____

_____

_____

Whose example will you choose to follow — the children of Israel's or Abraham's?

_____

_____

PRAYER

Lord, I realize that I've imitated the children of Israel in my walk with you. I've rebelled against you by not completely trusting you with this area of my life. I ask you to forgive me. I will strive diligently to seek your Word and become an imitator of those who, through adding faith to your promises and then waiting patiently, received the desires of their hearts. I know Your Word is true and that You reward those who diligently seek You. I have so much to gain from putting my absolute trust in Your faithfulness. I choose abundant life and put my trust in You! In Jesus' name I pray. Amen.

Lesson 14
Entering God's Rest

PURPOSE

To realize that God has prepared a place of rest for His people, and thereby gain a greater understanding of how to enter His rest. When you enter His rest, you'll receive all He has promised and you'll partake of the wonderful plan He has for your life.

OVERVIEW

You learned in the previous lesson that the children of Israel didn't enter God's rest because they didn't put their trust in Him. They didn't receive all He had promised them because they failed to enter His rest. This is why it's so important for you to understand what it means to "rest in God." The scriptures teach that you must enter God's rest in order to receive all He has promised. God has prepared a place of rest specifically for you. It's a place in your Christian life where you cast all your cares on Him and put your complete trust in His Word. When you put your trust in God, He is actively at work in your life bringing to pass His perfect plan for you.

DISCUSSION

Read Hebrews 4:1-16. *1Therefore, While the promise of entering His rest still holds and is offered [today], let us be afraid [to distrust it], lest any of you should think he has come too late and has come short of [reaching] it. 2For indeed we have had the glad tidings [Gospel of God] proclaimed to us just as truly as they [the Israelites of old did when the good news of deliverance from bondage came to them]; but the message they heard did not benefit them, because it was not mixed with faith (with the leaning of the entire personality on God in absolute trust and confidence in His power, wisdom, and goodness) by those who heard it; neither were they united in faith with the ones [Joshua and Caleb] who heard (did believe). 3For we who have believed (adhered to and trusted in and relied on God) do enter that rest, in accordance with His declaration that those [who did not believe] should not enter when He said, As I swore in My wrath, They shall not enter My rest; and this He said although [His] works had been completed and prepared [and waiting for all who would believe] from the foundation of the world. 4For in a certain place He has said this about the seventh day: And God rested on the seventh day from all His works. 5And they [forfeited their part in it, for] in this [passage] He said, They shall not enter My rest. 6Seeing then that the promise remains over [from past times] for some to enter that rest, and that those who formerly were given the good news about it and the opportunity, failed to appropriate it and did not enter because of disobedience, 7Again He sets a definite day, [a new] Today, [and gives another opportunity of securing that rest] saying through David after so long a time in the words already quoted, Today, if you would hear His voice and when you hear it do not harden your hearts. 8[This mention of a rest was not a reference to their entering into Canaan.] For if Joshua had given them rest, He [God] would not speak afterwards about another day. 9So then, there is still awaiting a full and complete Sabbath-rest reserved for the [true] people of God; 10For he who has once entered [God's] rest also has ceased from [the weariness and pain] of human labors, just as God rested from those labors peculiarly His own. 11Let us therefore be zealous and exert ourselves and strive diligently to enter that rest [of God, to know and experience it for ourselves], that no one may fail or perish by the same kind of unbelief and disobedience [into which those in the wilderness fell]. 12For the Word that God speaks is alive and full of power [making it active, operative, energizing, and effective]; it is sharper than any two-edged sword, penetrating to the dividing line of the breath of life (soul) and [the immortal] spirit, and of joints and marrow [of the deepest parts of our nature], exposing and sifting and analyzing and judging the very thoughts and purposes of the heart. 13And not a creature exists that is concealed from His sight, but all things are open and exposed, naked and defenseless to the eyes of Him with Whom we have to do. 14In-as-much then as we have a great High Priest Who has [already] ascended and passed through the heavens, Jesus the Son of God, let us hold fast our confession [of faith in Him]. 15For we do not have a High Priest Who is unable to understand and sympathize and have a shared feeling with our weaknesses and infirmities and liability to the assaults of temptation, but One Who has been tempted in every respect as we are, yet without sinning. 16Let us then fearlessly and confidently and boldly draw near to the throne of grace (the throne of God's unmerited favor to us sinners), that we may receive mercy [for our failures] and find grace to help in good time for every need [appropriate help and well-timed help, coming just when we need it].* (AMP)

Read Hebrews 4:1 again.

What does this scripture say is still being offered to you today? _____

_____

Let's review for a moment what it mean to enter God's rest. Look again at the definition of "rest" to get a clearer understanding of what it means to rest in God:

"Rest" means:
- freedom from anything that tires, troubles, or disturbs you
- to be free from care, worry and anxiety
- to have peace
- to rely, trust or depend on someone

Today, God is still offering the promise of entering His rest, just as He offered it to the children of Israel. This promise means God has pledged that by putting their complete trust in Him, His people can be free from worry, care, or fear concerning every area of their life. God's rest is a place where you're free from anything that tires, troubles, or disturbs you; a place where you have His perfect peace because you've put your absolute trust in Him.

In verse 1, what does God tell you to fear?_____

_____

This scripture tells you that you should be afraid **not** to trust God's promise of entering His rest. Recalling the definition of rest, then, this means you should be afraid to allow yourself to worry or be troubled concerning any situation. The reason this is so important is because in order to receive God's promises, **you must enter His rest** by putting your complete trust in Him. The Bible teaches that only those who put their absolute trust in God will inherit His promises (Hebrews 6:12). If you worry and become frustrated concerning your situation, you haven't put your trust in God and you aren't resting in Him. You learned in Lesson 13 that when you worry instead of trusting God, you set yourself apart from Him; you withdraw yourself from His protection and favor; you stand aloof from the living God and hinder His plan for you from coming to pass in your life. **Be afraid to worry!** The children of Israel didn't receive God's promises because they didn't enter His rest. Their unbelief shut them out. They chose to worry and be fearful rather than to trust God. They exalted their circumstances above the power of His promise; therefore, they didn't receive God's perfect plan for their lives.

James 1:6-7 says *6he who doubts is like a wave of the sea, blown and tossed by the wind. 7That man shall not think he will receive anything from the Lord.* (NIV)

What will keep you from receiving God's best?_____

_____

Worry is the result of doubt. It keeps God's blessings from flowing into your life. God commands us in Philippians 4:6: *Don't worry about anything; instead pray about everything.* (TLB)

How can you know if you've entered God's rest?

These characteristics will be present in your life when you've entered God's rest:

- You have God's perfect peace.

- You've put your trust in a promise of God concerning your situation.

- You're free from anything that tires, troubles, or disturbs you.

- You're confident that God is at work on your behalf even if you don't see anything happening in the natural.

- You rest in God's promise and don't try to figure out when, where, or how He will bring His promises to pass.

- Your faith isn't based on your circumstances; it's based on God's promise. You walk by faith not by sight.

- You exalt the power of God's promise above your circumstances.

These characteristics will be present in your life when you haven't entered God's rest:

- You're full of worry and concern.

- You doubt God's promises will really come to pass in your life.

- You're overwhelmed by your circumstances and feel like giving up.

- You are discouraged when your circumstances don't change quickly.

- You struggle to try to figure out how He is going to bring His promise to pass; you cannot rest.

- Your faith is determined by what you see. Your present circumstances cause you to doubt God's promise.

- You exalt your circumstances above the power of God's promise.

Have you entered God's rest? Which characteristics are present in your life? Have you put yourself in a position to receive His best, or are you allowing worry and doubt to keep you from receiving His perfect plan?

Examples of entering God's rest:

- When you enter God's rest concerning your finances, you're free from worry, care, and anxiety. You have His perfect peace because you know your Heavenly Father will take care of your every need. You cast your care on Him and replace it with His promise. You rest secure because you know your Heavenly Father will bring to pass His promise of financial abundance in your life.

- When you enter God's rest concerning your spouse, you no longer become frustrated and upset with them because they aren't doing what you want them to do. You have confidence that God will perfect that which concerns you. You're free from anything that troubles or disturbs you concerning your spouse. You see them through the eyes of faith; you know that they'll become the spouse that God wants. You're confident that He is at work in them creating the desire and ability to do what pleases Him. You're confident of what you hope for, and convinced of what you can't see. You know that God will bring to pass His perfect will and plan because nothing is impossible with Him.

Read Hebrews 4:2.

Why didn't the promise that God gave to the Israelites benefit their lives?_____

_____

The promises God gave the Israelites didn't benefit them because they didn't choose to put their absolute trust in His Word. They didn't mix faith with God's promise. You can know of God's promises; but if you don't put your complete trust in them, they won't benefit you. You won't, therefore, appropriate His blessings in your life. Many of God's people aren't seeing the fulfillment of His promises because they're making the same mistake the children of Israel made. They exalt their circumstances above the power of God's promise. They allow their circumstances to cause them to worry and doubt; they don't mix faith with what God has promised concerning their situation.

You've heard the good news of the Gospel of Jesus just as the children of Israel heard the good news of deliverance from bondage. You've heard that you're an heir to all the promises of God. No matter how many promises God has made, they all find their "yes" answer in Christ (II Corinthians 1:19-20). However, this good news won't benefit you if you don't mix it with what?

Read Hebrews 4:3.

Who will enter God's rest? How can you enter God's rest?_____

_____

When you completely trust God to work in you and for you, you'll enter His rest. God has promisedyou, as a new covenant believer, that He will not only fulfill His promises in your life, but He will also enable you to obey His Word. God will give you the desire and ability to do your part, and He will do His part. All He requires from you is that you completely trust Him.

Read Jeremiah 32:38-42.

What does God promise He will do in you? (verse 40)_____

_____

_____

What does God promise He will do for you? (verse 42)_____

_____

_____

God promises He will inspire you to fear Him. He will give you singleness of heart and action so that you'll obey Him. He will never stop doing good to you, and He will give you all the prosperity that He has promised. This is good news! Those who enter God's rest will receive this promise.

Absolute trust in God's Word will bring you to a position of rest. You'll have a confident assurance that God will perform what He has promised. When you believe this, you free yourself from fear, worry and concern, and your life becomes full of God's perfect peace. When you trust in God's Word for your every need or desire, you enter a place of rest. Hebrews 4:3 says that God's work, all that He has planned and prepared for us, has been waiting for those who will believe.

Now that you know what it means to rest, what attitudes or actions in your own life reveal unrest?_____

_____

_____

Fear, frustration, worry, concern, anxiety, discouragement, stress and doubt are all characteristics of a person who hasn't entered God's rest. Do you have some of these characteristics in your own life? Explain._____

_____

_____

Read Hebrews 4:4-6.

How did the Israelites forfeit their part in entering God's rest? What did they do that caused them not to appropriate this promise in their lives?_____

_____

How can you forfeit your part in entering God's rest?_____

_____

These verses reveal that the promise of entering God's rest is still available to you today. You can enter in and appropriate it in your life by choosing to put your absolute trust in His Word, or you can follow the example of the children of Israel and fail to enter His rest by choosing to worry instead of trusting Him. This promise was given to the children of Israel, but they didn't enter because of disobedience and unbelief.

Read Hebrews 4:7.

What is God giving you another opportunity to do?_____

_____

Every day God gives you another opportunity to enter His rest. Every day is a new "today." God is patient with you because He loves you. He will never give up on you. He wants you to completely put your trust in the promises He has given in His Word. However, if you've failed, He gives you another opportunity to secure that rest. He says *today* if you'll put your absolute trust in Me, you can enter My rest. Make a decision today to put your absolute trust in God's promises and enter that place of rest that He has prepared and waiting for you.

According to verse 7, what does God say you shouldn't do when you hear His Word?

_____

This scripture is saying that when you hear God's Word, don't harden your heart to it. You learned in Lesson 13 that the children of Israel rebelled against God by hardening their hearts to His Word. The children of Israel rebelled against God in two ways.
  1. They chose to worry instead of trusting in God's promise.
  2. They wouldn't obey God's Word.

You should be afraid to follow their example.

Be aware that when you worry instead of trusting God, you're rebelling against Him. He has specifically instructed you to trust Him. When you don't do this, you're disobeying Him.

Read Hebrews 4:8-10.

In verse 10, how does God describe the full, complete Sabbath rest that He has reserved for His people?_____

_____

_____

God says there is a complete Sabbath rest reserved for His people who will believe His Word. When you enter His rest, you cease from your own efforts and let Him take control of your situation. God reserved six days for work. He left one day for rest, relaxing from labor. However, God's rest is an every day, complete rest that you receive by casting all your care, all your anxieties, and all your worries on Him, resting in His love and faithfulness to His Word. If you cast your burdens on the Lord and rest in His promises, He will take care of your future and fulfill every promise in your life.

In Matthew 11:28-29 Jesus says, 28*"Come to Me, all you who are weary and burdened, and I will give you rest.* 29*...learn from Me...and you will find rest for your souls."* (NIV)

You'll find your mind and your emotions at rest if you'll come to Jesus and learn from God's Word. You can be free from fear and worry about each situation in your life if you'll give it to Jesus and put your absolute trust in what He has promised.

Read Hebrews 4:11.

What two things kept the Israelites from entering God's rest and receiving His promise?

1. _____

2. _____

According to verse 11, what do you need to do to experience God's rest for yourself? Why is it so important that you enter God's rest? _____

_____

_____

_____

"Zealous" means full of enthusiastic diligence; an eager desire.
"Exert" means to put oneself into strenuous vigorous action or effort.
"Strive" means to struggle vigorously.

Consider these words carefully so that you can fully understand how very important it is to God that you enter His rest. You can't be slothful about God if you truly want to receive all the promises He has provided for you.

How can you get to that place of rest?

In Lesson 10, you learned the process that brings you to a position of being able to completely trust in God.

In Proverbs 22:17-19, you discovered four steps that will bring you to a place of complete rest in God:

1. Listen and submit to God's Word.
2. Meditate on the knowledge of God.
3. As you meditate on God's Word, it will enter into your heart and you'll begin to believe it. You'll rejoice in what God has promised.
4. Your lips will be accustomed to confessing God's promises.

These scriptures say that doing these things will bring you to a place of complete trust in God. You must be full of enthusiastic diligence, and have an eager desire to seek God's Word so you can know what He has promised you. It takes effort to reach the place where you can completely trust God. Search His Word and meditate on His promises. Speaking God's Word over your situation to overcome temptations of doubt, fear and worry. Cast down every imagination that exalts itself above the knowledge of God's Word. Once God's Word has truly entered your heart and you begin to completely trust in Him, you'll enter into God's rest.

Read Hebrews 4:12.

How does this scripture describe God's Word? _____

_____

God's Word is full of power. It's alive, active, energizing and effective. That's why you should seek the knowledge of His Word as though it were silver and gold. When you enter God's rest by putting your absolute trust in His Word, it has the power to heal your marriage, heal your body, deliver you from trouble, fulfill the desires of your heart, bring your family to salvation, and fill your life with all of His wonderful blessings. God's Word will never fail those who put their absolute trust in it.

I Thessalonians 2:13 says: *And we (especially) thank God for this, that when you received the message of God (which you heard) from us, you welcomed it not as the word of (mere) men but as what it truly is, **the Word of God**, which is effectually at work in you who believe—exercising its (superhuman) power in those who **adhere to** and **trust in** and **rely on it**.* (AMP)

This scripture clearly shows that when you receive the Bible for what it truly is, the Word of God, it will exercise its supernatural power in your situation if you'll adhere to, trust in and rely on it concerning every area of your life.

Read Hebrews 4:13.

Can you hide anything from God? Does He know your heart? Can He read your thoughts?

_____

God knows everything about you; you can't hide anything from Him; He knows the motives of your heart. You can fool those around you but you can never fool God. He knows whether or not you're truly trusting in His Word. God is the only one who knows whether a person has entered His rest.

Read Hebrews 4:14.

Who is your great High Priest?_____

You're to hold fast to what?_____

When you confess your faith in Jesus, you're putting your trust in what He has provided for you. **Your confession of faith is what you confidently expect God to do about your situation according to a promise that He has given you in His Word.**

What is your confession of faith concerning your situation?

1. _____
2. _____
3. _____
4. _____
5. _____

Read Hebrews 4:15.

Does Jesus understand your struggles and your weaknesses? Does He understand your temptations to be worried and concerned? Why does He understand? How can He know how it feels to be tested and tried in your faith?_____

_____

_____

Jesus has compassion. He understands how it feels to be tested, and how it feels to go through trials. However, I Corinthians 10:13 says: *There hath no temptation taken you but such as is common to man: but God is faithful, who will not suffer you to be tempted above that ye are able; but will with the temptation also make a way to escape, that ye may be able to bear it.* (KJV)

What is the way of escape? What has God given you so you can escape temptation? Jesus escaped temptation so that you could follow His example.

In Matthew 4:1-11, Jesus' faith was tried; however, every time the devil tempted Him, He spoke God's Word and it gave Him strength to overcome every temptation. In this same way, you can escape the temptation to doubt, worry or become discouraged concerning your situation. When the devil comes to tempt you, begin to speak out the promises of God that you're standing on. If you'll do it in boldness, you'll also be victorious over temptation. You'll walk in victory in every area of your life.

Read Hebrews 4:16.

What should you do when you're tempted to surrender to your circumstances and give up under trial? What should you do when you feel yourself falling from God's rest? What will God do for you?_____

_____

_____

_____

Many times, when you enter God's rest by putting your absolute trust in His promises, trials (circumstances) tempt you to begin to worry and fret over the situation once again. When you feel yourself falling from that place of rest, you can come boldly and confidently before God's throne of grace to receive mercy for your failures and find grace to help you in your time of need. God will give you the strength to stand strong. He will never give up on you. Every day He gives you another opportunity to enter into His rest and walk in abundant life. When you rest in God, you've put your complete trust in Him.

SUMMARY

The Bible teaches that you should be afraid to doubt the promise about entering God's rest. You must enter His rest in order to receive all He has planned for you. Be aware that when you doubt God's Word and worry about your situation, you keep yourself from receiving what He has promised. Those who put their absolute trust in Him, who depend on His grace and confidently expect His promises to come to pass in their lives, have entered His rest. They're free from worry, fear and care concerning their situation because they have God's perfect peace. Be zealous — exert yourself and strive diligently to enter God's rest. It takes effort to seek God, to meditate upon His promises, and to cast down imaginations that contradict His Word. Every day, God gives you another opportunity to enter His rest. He is quick to forgive when you fail. You can come boldly to the throne of grace to receive mercy for your failures and to find grace to help you in your time of need. God loves you, and He wants to do exceeding abundantly above your highest prayers, desires, thoughts, hopes or dreams. All He requires from you is that you completely trust Him and enter into His rest.

PERSONAL APPLICATION

Explain the situations you are facing.

1. _____

_____

2. _____

_____

Which promises of God are you trusting Him to perform in your life?
Situation #1

    a. _____

    b. _____

    c. _____

    d. _____

    e. _____

Situation #2

    a. _____

    b. _____

    c. _____

    d. _____

    e. _____

SELF-EXAMINATION

Have you entered God's rest concerning these situations? Are you resting in His promises?
_____

Are you free from worry, doubt, and care concerning these situations? Do you have God's perfect peace?_____

Are you free from anything that tires, troubles, or disturbs you?_____

Are you free from trying to figure out how or when God is going to bring His promises to pass?_____

Are you free from trying to help God do something that only He can do?_____

Do you have a vision of God's promises coming to pass in your life?_____

Are you confidently claiming God's promises to be true in your life?_____

Are you confident of what you hope for and convinced of what you can't see?_____

_____

If you can answer "yes" to all of these questions, you've entered God's rest. You're in a position to receive God's perfect will in your life.

If you can't honestly answer "yes" to all of these questions, then remember that you must trust in God's grace to do the work inside you as you meditate on His Word.

REVIEW QUESTIONS

1. What should you be afraid to distrust? (Hebrews 4:1)_____

2. Why did God's people fail to receive His promises?_____

3. How can you enter God's rest? (Hebrews 4:3; Proverbs 22:17-19)_____

   _____

   _____

   _____

   _____

4. Why is it so important to enter God's rest?_____

   _____

Read Matthew 14:25-33. In this passage you can see another example of entering God's rest and how He will help if you begin to fall. Answer the following questions about this passage.

The disciples were out on a boat in the middle of the night and Jesus came to them, walking on the water in the midst of a storm. The disciples were afraid and Jesus said, "Stop being afraid!" Peter said, "Lord, if it is you, command me to come to you on the water." What word of God was Peter trusting in when he stepped out of the boat? (verse 29)

_____

Which promises in God's Word are you standing on?_____

_____

_____

_____

Notice that when Peter got that word from Jesus, he forgot about the storm and began walking out on the promise. At that moment, Peter put His trust in Jesus' Word and walked on the water toward Him. When you put your trust in God, you take your eyes off the storm going on around you (the situation you've been worrying about — the circumstances in your life that look impossible), and you begin to rest in God's promise.

As long as Peter kept His eyes on Jesus (God's Word) and the promise He had given him, he was at peace and walked on the water. But what happened in verse 30?

_____

Peter began to look back at the storm going on all around him (his circumstances began to look bigger than God's Word) and he began to sink. The moment he began to doubt, he was overwhelmed by his circumstances.

You can apply this to your own life: Are you looking at your problem, wondering if it's too big for your God to work out? Or are you keeping your eyes on Jesus (God's promise) and the fact that no situation is impossible for Him?_____

Are you sinking in your trials or are you walking on water? Did Peter allow himself to drown in his circumstances? How can you be strengthened when you feel yourself falling from resting in God's promises? (verse 30)_____

_____

As Peter was sinking (falling from rest), He cried out. He came boldly before Jesus and cried out for help, "Lord, save me from destruction!" How long did it take Jesus to help Peter? (verse 31)_____

Jesus instantly reached out His hand to help Peter in his trouble. Peter cast his burden back on Jesus, and Jesus sustained him, supported him and carried him through the storm. What question did Jesus ask Peter? (verse 31)_____

_____

When you get your eyes off of God's Word and on what's concerning you, you're doubting God's promise. However, if you'll look back to Jesus and what He has promised, He will reach out His hand to wherever you are, pull you back to that place of rest, and carry you through your trial to victory. Isn't that exactly what He did with Peter? What happened when they got back in the boat? (verses 32-33)_____

_____

_____

The storm was over, the trial had ceased and there was victory. You'll have victory in your life concerning every problem you face if you will hold fast to God's promises and keep your eyes on Him. He will never fail to fulfill His promises if you'll completely trust Him. He will watch over His Word and perform it in your life!

Epilogue
My Personal Testimony —
Looking to God's Promises in the
Midst of a Troubled Marriage

I'd always heard people say that the first couple of years of marriage are the hardest. But, after six years I continued to struggle in my marriage. Instead of getting better, things seemed to grow worse. I tried to be a good wife but I always seemed to fail. My husband and I were both Christians, yet strife filled our home. We couldn't seem to get along. I was very unhappy with my marriage, and many times I was discouraged because I felt as though it might never change. I'd prayed, but my faith was weak. I'd heard people teach that each person has a will and even though you pray for them, God won't change their will. How hopeless that message made me feel!

Thoughts of divorce ran through my mind many times, but I knew that wasn't the answer. It wasn't the solution to my problem.

One day after a huge fight with my husband, I felt as though I couldn't deal with the situation anymore. I hated my marriage, and my husband had expressed that he felt that way, too. I knew I couldn't live like that. As I sat down in my chair, I picked up my Bible and began to weep. I cried out to God, "God, please help me. I know the answer I need is in Your Word. Please help me find it. "

As I prayed, I asked the Holy Spirit to guide me to the truth I needed. The gospel was supposed to be good news. I knew the Bible says "you shall know the Truth and the Truth will set you free." I prayed, "Lord, I submit myself to You. I'll follow Your counsel and I'll trust in Your Word." I knew the answer I needed could be found somewhere there in the Word of God.

As I opened my Bible, the first scripture I remember reading was I John 5:14-15. It said that I could have confidence that God would answer my prayer if I prayed according to His will. It didn't say my prayer had to be according to my husband's will, **but according to God's will**. Hope began to rise in my heart as I thought about that scripture. Then I thought, "Now all I need to know is God's will for my marriage." I began to search God's Word for every scripture I could find on husbands and wives.

I discovered Proverbs 31:10-31, Ephesians 5:21-33, I Peter 3:1-12 and I Corinthians 13:4-8. In these scriptures, God revealed to me what His perfect will was for my marriage. I wanted God's best. I wanted the marriage that God wanted me to have — but it seemed so impossible to me. Then the Holy Spirit reminded me of Luke 1:37 which says, *For with God nothing is ever impossible and no word from God shall be without power or impossible of fulfillment.* I realized that with God it was possible for these scriptures to come to pass in my life. If I prayed God's Word, I would be praying His will. According to I John 5:14-15, I then could have confidence and know that God would answer my prayer. This promise became my source of strength.

I wanted to be the wife that Scripture showed me I should be, but I realized that I'd failed miserably. I humbled myself before God and asked Him to forgive me. I knew that in my own strength I couldn't love my husband the way God's Word told me to; sometimes I felt as though I didn't even like him. I could only see his wrongs, his weaknesses, his selfishness — and he could only see and talk about what was wrong with me. We blamed each other for our marital problems.

But as I continued to seek God, the Holy Spirit led me to another scripture, Philippians 2:13, which says it is *not in your own strength, for it is God who is all the while effectually at work in you (energizing and creating in you the power and desire), both to will and to work for His good pleasure, satisfaction and delight.* I realized that if I would depend on God, He would create in me and my husband the desire and ability to love each other with His unconditional love. What a miracle that would be, because I didn't feel like walking in love toward my husband.

I prayed I Corinthians 13:4-7 over myself: "Heavenly Father, I want to follow Your counsel because I know it will produce your blessings in my life. I ask you to create in me the desire and ability to love my husband with Your love. I ask you to give me the strength to be patient and kind toward him. Help me to not be easily angered. With your help I won't take account of the wrongs done to me. Help me see the best in him, and see him through your eyes. Lord, change me into the wife that you want me to be."

I prayed for wisdom on how to handle my husband's moods. I needed God's strength to do it His way. The Holy Spirit led me to I Peter 3:9-11, Proverbs 15:1 and Ephesians 4:29-32. As I depended on the Holy Spirit, He helped me respond to negative words the way God had instructed. With my eyes on God's promise (I John 5:14-15), I had strength to obey God. I knew He would answer my prayer and perform His will in my marriage.

Then I began to pray God's Word over my husband. And as I did, faith rose within my heart. I knew God would change me, and I knew He would change my husband. I prayed Ephesians 5:25 and I Corinthians 13:4-7 over him: "Heavenly Father, I ask You to create in my husband the desire and ability to love me like Christ loves the Church. I ask You to develop Your unconditional love inside him toward me. Create in him the desire and ability to be patient and kind, never proud or selfish. I pray that he would not be easily angered. I ask that he would begin to see the best in me."

One scripture I continued to pray over him was Proverbs 31:28-30. I thanked God for His promise that if I would reverently fear Him (obey His Word), my husband would begin to think that I was the greatest wife in the world. How impossible that scripture seemed! But the Holy Spirit revealed to me in Mark 9:23 that nothing was impossible if I would only believe.

God also revealed to me, in Ephesians 6:10-18 that I must draw my strength from Him and His Word. He showed me I must put on His whole armor to stand successfully against the strategies and deceits of the devil. I realized that the devil came to steal, kill and destroy my marriage, but that Jesus came so I could enjoy life and have it in abundance. My Heavenly Father wanted me to experience abundant life in my marriage.

Ephesians 6:12 showed me that my fight wasn't against my husband; he wasn't the problem. My fight was against principalities, against the powers of darkness and the spiritual forces of evil. The way I could be victorious was by speaking God's Word over my marriage; and as I fully trusted in God, I would defeat all the fiery darts of the enemy. I rejoiced as I realized "greater is He who is in me than he who is in the world." (I John 4:4)

God's Word wouldn't fail me, for it's alive and full of power. It's operative, energizing and effective. Effective means that God's Word will produce the desired result. (Hebrews 4:16 AMP)

Every day I built my faith as I praised and thanked God for what He was doing in our hearts toward one another. Never again would I believe that God won't change a person's heart, because Proverbs 21:1 says that God will change the heart of a king; and if He will do that, He can change anyone. I realized that the message I had heard came from lack of knowledge.

Hosea 4:6 says that God's people are destroyed for lack of knowledge. Through lack of knowledge many Christian marriages fail. How this must grieve the Holy Spirit, for in Malachi 2:16 it says that God hates divorce. The devil can destroy when God's people are wrongly taught.

As I thanked God for His promise and continued to speak His Word over my husband, my outward circumstances didn't change immediately. But my trust grew dramatically. I knew God would keep His promise. Jeremiah 1:12 says that God is alert and active watching over His Word to perform it. I knew He would perform His perfect will in my marriage as I trusted Him.

When I realized what God wanted for me, and that He promised to perform His will in my life, I was determined to receive His best. Nothing or no one could discourage me from believing that God's plan would come to pass in my life. I was committed to loving my husband no matter what I had to face. I knew God's love wouldn't fail to produce the desired result.

As the days went by, I faced challenging circumstances that tested my faith; but with the help of the Holy Spirit, I continued to keep my eyes on God's promise and the hope it offered me. My whole attitude toward my husband began to change and a new love grew within my heart. With God's help I was able to react to anger His way. The first sign in the natural that God was at work in my husband happened about a month later. I hadn't told my husband what God had shown me, but one day He said, "Do you know what's been on my heart to pray lately?" I asked "What?" and he replied, "I've been praying that I would love you like Christ loves the Church." I almost cried as I realized how faithful

God is to His Word. He was indeed at work in my husband, creating in him the power and desire to love me with His unconditional love.

It has been over five years since that day, and God has continued to prove Himself faithful. Ephesians 3:20 has come to pass in my life. It says that according to the power of God that is at work in me, God is able to do exceedingly above all that I could ever hope, dream, or desire.

I admire, respect, and deeply love my husband. He's the godly father and husband that I wanted him to be. He continually says, "You're the greatest wife in the world!" God has done a miracle in my marriage. He watched over His Word and performed it in my life. Our home, which was once filled with anger and strife, is now filled with God's love, His joy, and His peace. I continue to thank God for the work that He has done and is continuing to do. As I continue to trust Him, He will continue to work in us and develop that good work, perfect it, and bring it to completion until the day of Christ's return. (Philippians 1:6)

Your marriage may not be as unhappy as mine was; but, you may still desire a deeper love between you and your spouse. On the other hand, your marriage may be much worse. You must realize that there's no situation that's too difficult for God. If you'll be committed to following God's counsel, and if you'll trust in His promises, you'll also experience His wonderful plan for your marriage. You, too, will be a living testimony that God is faithful to His Word.

Divorce is never the right answer for a troubled marriage. Jesus is the only answer. The devil will try and convince you that divorce is the easy way out. But if you choose divorce, you'll go from relationship to relationship never finding the love you so desperately want, because human love can never bring true happiness and joy. The only love that completely satisfies is God's love. His unconditional love is the only love that will never fail you. He is able to develop His love within you and your spouse as you completely trust in Him. If you're ever to receive the marriage that God has planned for you, you must make a commitment to His Word. You must know that your Heavenly Father loves you and wants you to have the best. All He's waiting for is for you to completely submit your life to Him and trust in His Word. You mustn't take the "I'll try this and see if it works" attitude, for you'll surely fail and give up. Only when you're determined to do it God's way will you begin to experience real victory in your life.

AFTERWORD

The most precious promise that God has given us is eternal life through His Son, Jesus Christ. It is important that you understand that all of God's other blessings come to us only through Jesus. John 3:16 tells us *"God so loved the world that He gave His only begotten Son that whosoever believeth in Him shall not perish but have eternal life."*

If you have never received God's promise of eternal life through faith in Jesus, it's as simple as saying a heartfelt prayer.

Romans 10:9-10 tells us *"if you confess with your mouth Jesus as Lord, and believe in your heart that God has raised Him from the dead, you shall be saved; for with the heart man believes, resulting in righteousness, and with the mouth he confesses, resulting in salvation."*

If you've never asked Jesus Christ to be the Lord of you life and would like to do so, then pray this prayer out loud:

Heavenly Father, I believe that Jesus died for my sins and rose again. I ask you, Lord Jesus, to come into my heart and be the Lord of my life. I ask you to forgive me and cleanse me from my sins. Thank you for your promise of eternal life. In Jesus' name, Amen

To contact the author, please write:

Connie Witter
P.O. Box 3064
Broken Arrow, OK 74013-3064

WE WANT TO KNOW WHAT YOU THINK ABOUT THIS STUDY!

Please share your comments
or suggestions with us at:

editorial@hensleypublishing.com

Toll Free Ordering: 800.288.8520
Fax: 918.664.8562
Phone: 918.664.8520

Order Online for Extra Savings!
www.hensleypublishing.com

HENSLEY
PUBLISHING

6116 E 32nd St
Tusa Ok 74135